ISLE OF MAN TT GREATS

IN THEIR OWN WORDS

To Lewis
A true TT fan!

ISLE OF MAN TT GREATS

IN THEIR OWN WORDS

TT '25

VOLUME ONE

DAVE MOORE

First published in Great Britain in 2023 by Mwyllin Publishing

ISBN 978-1-3999-5397-9

British Library Cataloguing-in-Publication Data
A catalogue record for this book is available from the British Library

Cover photograph © Don Morley
Cover design by Kit Nelson
Typesetting by Heather Bowen

Printed in the UK with production managed by Ink & Roller.

CONTENTS

INTRODUCTION

Anyone who takes part in the Isle of Man TT races deserves to be labelled 'great', from the World champions to the multiple-Mountain course winners and the lap record holders plus the part-time riders who often make up the lower numbers at the back of the grid. That's because of the challenge they take on. There really is nothing quite like the Isle of Man TT. Its uniqueness is just part of its mass appeal. A mammoth thirty-seven and three-quarter miles of twisting roads containing an estimated 264 bends, connected by flat-out straights lined with walls, hedges, banks, trees, houses, everything you expect to see on normal everyday roads with their humps, lumps and bumps.

Nothing else like it on the planet.

Nothing.

Other races like the North West 200 and the Ulster Grand Prix in Northern Ireland plus the Macau Grand Prix in Asia are amazing and thrilling events in their own right but run on shorter courses. Logic would suggest that mass start racing would have more appeal than a time trial yet it's the nature of what the Isle of Man TT is about that separates it from anything else. I've been fortunate to commentate on all four events plus many others and the TT is the one that requires the most work. It also has a history unmatched by any other motorcycle event, arguably across the whole of motorsport. Woods, Duke, McIntyre, Surtees, Hailwood, Agostini, Dunlop, Hislop, Jefferies, McGuinness, not only 'greats' but 'legends'. No-one can argue with that. Everything that's needed to be written about these TT behemoths has been done so. There's nothing more I can add. As a fan, what I want to know are the unknown stories, the tales rarely heard, the memories that deserve to be shared. Each of the riders featured in this book have either won a TT or a Manx Grand Prix race (or in the case of Murray Walker, the son of a TT winner).

Welcome to Isle of Man TT Greats Volume One.

GIACOMO AGOSTINI

Born Brescia, Italy

TT Years 1965-1972
10 x wins, 1 x 2nd, 1 x 3rd, 3 x DNF

Giacomo Agostini is more than a TT hero; he's a legend. Arguably, the first continental superstar of motorcycle racing. The archetypal Italian playboy. He arrived in the Isle of Man in 1965, bagged a podium finish and took his first TT win the year after. Twelve months later he was part of one of the greatest motorcycle races ever let alone at the Isle of Man when he and great friend and rival Mike Hailwood diced with one another in the Senior Jubilee race, the lead changing hands between them on numerous occasions. When Hailwood retired from racing Agostini was virtually unchallenged as he racked up TT wins and World Championship titles. His love affair with the Isle of Man came to an end in 1972 following the death of compatriot Gilberto Parlotti and he never raced there again. He still receives a hero's welcome whenever he returns to the Island, be it as guest of honour or just to take part in the parade lap.

When I was a young boy I read something about the Isle of Man before it was part of the World championship and there were a lot of Italians riding at the TT. I started racing when I was 15 years old and from that time I knew about the Isle of Man.

Growing up I had two or three heroes. Tarquinio Provini was one, so too was Carlo Ubbiali who was 9 times world champion. I also admired Gary Hocking. These were the people racing before I did so they were the ones I looked up to. I didn't see a lot of them because during this time there was not so much television therefore I had to find out about them in the newspapers.

I went to the TT for the first time in 1965 and it made a big impression on me because when I arrived in the Isle of Man and I saw the circuit I just thought it's impossible to learn. Before the races, I spent two weeks on the Island, travelling alone with my car and I went to the local dealer and rented a bike. I started in the morning at 9.30 and finished at 12 o'clock. I started again at 2 o'clock and finished at 4 each time, just going around to learn the circuit because it's very difficult to remember everything. I thought it would take me 2 years because the first year, even with lots and lots of practice, I still couldn't remember everything. Of course, I was going fast because if you go slow then it would be easier but It would take longer to know where you can go quickly.

Before I went, some people told me that it is a very long circuit, that it is very difficult, very dangerous and you must remember everything. Therefore, I decided to go and spend a fortnight on the Island before the Grand Prix to learn the circuit. Maybe Spa-Francorchamps in Belgium or the Nurburgring in Germany and even the Ulster Grand Prix are similar but the Isle of Man is much more difficult. There were good riders in 1965 too. Jim Redman, Mike Hailwood, Phil Read, these were big champions.

That first year at the TT I finished third. I remember Phil Read passed me in a place where I went down 2 gears. When I saw him the next time I tried to go faster and in that place I think I made up 3 or 4 seconds. But this is what I said before: you need time to learn and to go fast.

I learned a lot in my first year in the Isle of Man and thought about it quite often so when I went back in 1966 I felt ready, I knew everything I needed to as I had my book with my notes in, which I constantly read during the winter so I learned what I had to. In 1966, I was prepared plus I had a good bike as well as knowing my way around the circuit and I think this is why I won that year.

I think winning the Isle of Man for the rider is the best, it's the best victory. It is like winning the World Championship because winning there is completely everything. The only concern is the danger, you can't make a mistake because if you do, it can be very bad.

In the Isle of Man you have to ride at 100%. This is very important as it's very, very difficult to remember everything because when you have practice you only have 3 or 4 laps. Imagine today, Valentino Rossi or any other rider doing just 3 or 4 laps in one circuit. Nowadays, when we go to the normal circuit we do between 100 to 150 laps before the race and in the Isle of Man you do 5 or 6 laps before the race. This is what makes the Isle of Man different.

I was very lucky that I crashed only one time and it was the same place where Mike Hailwood crashed. We crashed together because there's water on the floor, the surface was wet. Both Mike and I passed at exactly the same place and we both crashed. As I said before you cannot crash at the Isle of Man so you must concentrate.

I didn't win the Senior TT in 1967 but this is one race I remember and I will remember for all my life because at that time I was leading by about 8 seconds in front of Mike Hailwood. So, for me it is a dream because I think not many riders can beat Mike Hailwood in the Isle of Man. That day I was dreaming of victory because I was only about 3 miles from the finish and the end of the lap when I broke my chain. I remember after the race I was crying because, of course, I had lost a very important race. Then Mike came to me, took me to a party and he said,

"You win today. I win but you are the winner."

This was very nice for me to hear. He was very nice with me and I remember also during the race I had a 3 or 4 second lead then Mike had a 2 or 3 second lead. It was a very hard race and after 360 kilometres I was leading but didn't finish. Anyway, this was still a very, very good race and everybody remembers this.

To win in the Isle of Man is very important because it's an important race. It is very difficult to race and because it is very dangerous, when you finish, you're very happy because the Isle of Man has everything whether it's a first gear corner, sixth gear corner, over 250 kilometres. You have the hairpin, you have got the Mountain then you go down again, so you have everything there. When you win it is because you are perfect.

I love the Isle of Man. I loved winning the TT. Everybody loved the TT but I thought it was too dangerous. I felt it had to change and I pushed many times to have it change. I spoke with the people who organised the event and the Isle of Man Government to say *'why don't you make a permanent short circuit'* because I remember before we had so many people come to the Isle of Man. Now it's not so many. I think it is important to bring back the World Championship to the Isle of Man but, of course, not in this condition. The GP riders today don't want to see the Isle of Man because as I said, when you crash you have little chance. Today the riders are on modern circuits where many people crash and stand up and go again. In the Isle of Man when you crash it is difficult to go again.

I didn't think it would still be going today. No-one races on the old circuits in all of Europe so it's a surprise there is still permission for racing on the Isle of Man. I'm very surprised because every year it seems some people die. This is not good for the sport and is also not good for the factory or the motorcycle. It is not good publicity because people want to buy the motorcycle but the family can lose a son. When you see and when you read about all these accidents, it does not help. I do hope one day the Isle of Man decides to build a new circuit, maybe keep the grandstand and the same tradition but with a new track, maybe seven or eight miles, perhaps 10 miles. There is a lot of space in the Isle of Man for this size. I think it's very nice because the Grand Prix should go back to the Isle of Man and with big success.

The speed now is incredible. To think about racing at an average of 125mph. Can you imagine racing at 170, 180 miles per hour on the normal road? A normal road where 10 minutes after the race you see the everyday cars and bicycles, where there's just been racing bikes going at 200 miles an hour.

When I go back I have watched the race at Bray Hill but I like to watch

"The speed now is incredible. To think about racing at an average of 125mph. Can you imagine racing at 170, 180 miles per hour on the normal road?"

GIACOMO AGOSTINI

the start because I always have emotion. It's very exciting, it brings back good memories because I think it is one of the best races.

When I go to the Isle of Man it is like I go to my home because the people are so nice to me and I have a nice memory of the Island. Of course, when I go to the Isle of Man I'm happy but at the same time I'm not happy because I think about my past. I think about when I used to race and I miss that. So I'm happy and not happy because I'm glad to see the circuit to see where I spent a lot of time, many years in the Isle of Man with practice in the morning at 04.45 when it started like this. There would be the lady in white, Gwen Crellin, waiting for me at Ballaugh to give me a cup of tea and this is a nice atmosphere. I think I will never, never forget the Isle of Man, for sure.

Now, the Isle of Man is for the specialist rider because the people know the circuit very well. Maybe these people live very close, maybe these people go many times to the Isle of Man. I think in the Isle of Man you see some people maybe finish first or second or third or fifth and maybe go to the Grand Prix and finish in 25th. The Isle of Man is a special race so these people know the Isle of Man and they are specialists who like road races. I think all these people are fantastic because every year or every 2 or 3 years something special happens. The speed is very, very good and impressive. Of course, when I see all the riders coming together after the finish line and when I see their faces it brings joy. Then you look at the hands and the blisters and it's because you need a lot of effort and a lot of power to finish all the 6 laps.

I only raced MV Agusta in the Isle of Man. For the TT it was very important to prepare the bike because we needed some special things. We needed a dampener to race Isle of Man where we didn't need it at other circuits. We also needed a longer swingarm, five centimetres longer so there was a certain way to set up the bike for the Isle of Man and nowhere else. For me, the 500cc 3-cylinder was the best. The 350cc 3-cylinder was special too. In the Isle of Man you need everything just right, especially the frame and its setting because the circuit is so different. Sometimes, one part is okay but not another part. Maybe when you set up the bike in one part the bike is not perfect, so you must have a compromise when you prepare. This is important to prepare the bike. It is impossible to have 100% because in some places you can go 100%, maybe in some other places only 70% perhaps it's different asphalt, a different situation. This is why you must have the compromise and prepare the bike for all the circuit because this is 64 kilometres which is 37 miles. You must have the bike not perfect but in good shape for good performance everywhere.

The circuit is a lot different because some corners are a little different and it's difficult to remember. There are times when I have ridden around it since I retired when I said *'where am I now, what do I do?'* This is difficult to know. It's many years of course and when you do only 1 lap it is difficult to remember.

I have a lot of memories. I have the circuit, this is a very, very nice memory. I have the race in '67 with Mike Hailwood which is very important for me. I will never forget the lady in white and she would be waiting for me every morning and she said hello. So I would stop and say hello and this is all these things which will never happen on another circuit. So this is why I say the Isle of Man is particularly special to me.

By the time he retired from racing, Giacomo Agostini had 122 Grand Prix wins and 15 World titles to his name, a feat no-one has so far managed to better. Like Surtees and Hailwood, Agostini dabbled with Formula One car racing but returned to motorcycle GPs as Marlboro Yamaha team manager. He oversaw Eddie Lawson win three 500cc titles during the 1980s. A short spell followed at Cagiva in the '90s and he finally retired from the paddock in 1995. He now lives in the hills above Bergamo in Italy.

KEL CARRUTHERS

Born Sydney, Australia 1938

TT Years 1966-70
19 races 2 wins, 1 x 2nd, 1 x 3rd, 2 x 5th, 1 x 6th, 1 x 7th, 1 x 10th, 1 x 11th, 2 x 12th, 7 x DNF

Kel Carruthers is a true motorcycle racing legend. He was not only a world champion and TT winner but went on to become one of the most successful engineers in the history of Grand Prix racing. He nurtured a young Kenny Roberts and helped groom him into a multiple world title winner and then looked after the bikes of legends such as Eddie Lawson. In an era when motorbike racing was extremely dangerous and taking place on less than safe circuits with death or serious injury a flick of the wrist away, Kel somehow survived 18 years of racing across his native Australia followed by Europe and America without breaking a single bone in his body or the need to visit hospital for treatment.

My dad's name was Jack Carruthers. He had a motorcycle shop and when he wasn't running that, he'd be competing as a Speedway sidecar rider. He started racing just before the war and when peace broke out he went on to become Australian champion a couple of times. He was recognised as the best Sidecar Speedway rider in the world at that time. Originally he had a 600 Manx Norton engine and then he was the first person to use

Vincent in the sidecars. In fact, in Australia, he ended up being called the Vincent man. So, I guess I was lucky being born into a motorcycle family. I must have been around 10 when I got my first little motorcycle. I was 12 when I started racing club events. The problem was you had to be 17 years old to get a competition licence. When I left school, I went to work for my dad who had a contract with the army to look after their 42 WLA Harleys and because of this we wangled a special street licence so I could do road tests as I was one of the mechanics.

I built my own bikes. I started off with BSA Bantams in the club events. My first competition race when I became a fully licensed rider was what we called short track. It's like a road race track only it's on dirt. I was 16. Things went well. I was a 'C' Grade rider and I won the 350 'C' Grade, the 350 'B' Grade, the 500 'B' Grade plus the 500 'C' Grade. I had a BSA B31 and I also rode dad's 500 Ariel. I finished fourth in the big race of the day with all the 'A' Grade riders and they immediately bumped me up to 'B' Grade. A good start to my racing career.

My first road race was at Bathurst, Mount Panorama. That was my introduction to Clubmans racing which meant you couldn't ride something like a proper Manx Norton so the best thing you could race was something like a Goldstar BSA or a Triumph. I had my dirt track bike, which was a 350 cast-iron BSA. I won the 'B' Grade Junior Clubmans so I was a winner in my first road race. I immediately made 'A' Grade after that and I just went on from there. I was the right size plus I guess I knew how to do it. Without seeming big-headed it seemed to come easy. I wasn't the best but I was at the front straight off. I was like, with it, you know.

Bathhurst then is basically the same as it is now except they didn't have the Armco barrier. It was a first class road race, a proper road racing track. Some people thought it was dangerous yet back in those days I'd often stated If you couldn't do good at Bathurst there's no point in going racing in Europe.

I learnt about the Isle of Man TT through buying magazines and we listened to the BBC broadcasts. They'd be about 10 minutes long with Graham Walker commentating. Through that I always wanted to go there, it was just the one to go to. There were lots of important races but the TT was the big one. This was the time of Geoff Duke and guys like that. There were some good Australians too, Keith Campbell and Jack Ahearn who would become a good friend of mine. I was a bit of an odd one out because back then kids didn't race motorcycles. So even when I was at school most of my friends were seven or eight years older than me as they were the riders at the race track. I lived in two different worlds but mainly my focus was on motorcycles.

Things went well enough that I was given the factory 250 four-cylinder Honda to race in Australia, which I did for five years. The last three years of that period I was winning everything, 250, 350, 500, every kind of race even though I was up against a lot of good riders, Jack Ahearn and all those guys, so by the time I went to Europe, I was the top Australian rider.

My dad sold the motorcycle shop so I needed to find something else to do. I met my wife Jan and we married when we were young. She has supported me all the way. One day we sat down, talked about going to Europe and just agreed, *'Hell, let's go'!*

We had two little kids by now and they went with us so they did this School in the Mailbox education system which was an Australian way of teaching kids in remote places. The first year was pretty difficult and a bit of a letdown because in my own mind, I was pretty well known. Due to all the results I'd had in Australia, there'd been plenty written about me in the English motorcycle papers. When I got to Europe, I found all these extra things I had never had to deal with before like carnets, which I needed so I could bring my stuff. I got rides at some of the races but quite often I didn't get my entry accepted because I hadn't done the grading races the year before.

When we moved to Europe I shipped everything. I had a 125 Honda plus a pair of Manx Nortons, one a 500 the other a 350. We lived in England where I bought a van and a caravan to live in. Back then you raced every weekend so you didn't really have a home to go to, you literally just went from one race meeting to the other. And in the off-season, in between my first and second year we rented a house close to Brands Hatch.

That first year, 1966, my mom and dad came over with me but in the caravan there was just me, my wife and our two kids.

One of the problems when I made my debut at the TT was the ferry strike. No boats were running during June so people couldn't get on or off the Isle of Man. It was put back until September. In the meantime we went to Northern Ireland, did the Ulster Grand Prix and then finally headed to the Isle of Man. When we arrived I think I might have managed to do one lap of the track in the van before practice started because the schedule was really condensed. I knew from the past, the other Aussie guys used to travel there two or three weeks before June and go round and round the track before practice started. I didn't have that luxury so it took a bit of learning; luckily I learned tracks pretty quick.

I kind of recognised some of it from photographs but I guessed what helped was the fact I wasn't young. I was 28 years of age. So I'd been around a bit. I didn't have that devil-may-care attitude you get in some youngsters. I was pretty smart at this point. I'm not sure which bike I rode for my first lap at the TT but it was probably the Norton. I was pretty excited, it was that kind of '*well, I'm finally here.*' I'd already done more than half a season of racing in Europe at that point so I was tuned into it all plus I'd raced for so long in Australia on the same equipment I now had.

I learned the TT course pretty well. I was smart enough to know that I could go fast where I could remember it properly and the other bits I wasn't so sure of I'd be more cautious. I did well that first year. I came 11th in the 500 class and 12th in the 125. My 350 broke on the first lap which was unfortunate. In the Isle of Man they used to lock the bikes away before the race and the 350 race was on the Wednesday. I took the bike out of the tent and up to the warm-up area but then the damn carburetor flooded like crazy. So we had to fix that which meant I never got the chance to warm the bike up before the start of the race. When I went to push off the grid for the start, the thing was just not ready to be raced so by the time I got to the bottom of Bray Hill the bike was starting to tighten up on me. I was unfortunate because I would have done better on the 350 than on the 500 because it's a little bit easier to ride.

I liked the Isle of Man from the off. I realised it was dangerous. I knew it would take me a couple of years before I could really do well there. We'd decided when we moved to Europe we would give it two years and see how it went. Thankfully, it went well and by the end of that second year I was one of the top privateers so we just kept going. That first time at the TT a friend of ours had a boarding house in Douglas, so we stayed there. It was close to the seafront so I'd ride up to the paddock from there as did, in fact, most of the other riders. The Island was buzzing too, there were lots of people wandering around through Douglas with its little narrow streets, full of shops. They were fun times, they got good crowds back in those days too. I've been back since I've retired and it really hasn't changed. Even today, it's kind of much the same as it used to be, especially around the paddock which isn't like what you'd find at a purpose-built racetrack.

At the end of my first season in Europe, I went to the Aermacchi factory to buy a bike. I picked it up in the new year, which was probably the best thing I ever did as it was very good. I went on to have some great results on it which put me in a good position with the Aermacchi factory. In fact, I did so well that people started showing up at the factory to get the same Aermacchi as I had. That bike took me to 10th in the Junior TT and I finished 5th on the 125, the little CR93 which was a great bike. However, I did have some pretty bad luck in the Isle of Man in one way or another. Everyone remembers the Senior TT battle between Mike Hailwood and Giacomo Agostini in 1967 but I'm damned if I do even if I was in it! I don't remember what happened that year, to be honest. I did alright in the 125, the 350 plus both 250 races but I just don't remember what happened on the 500. I knew both of those guys by this time, in fact when I first arrived in the paddock the top boys knew who I was so I got along well with them from the off. I got to know Mike Hailwood well and Jim Redman I'd already met in Australia when he raced there. No-one really hung out with one another. Back in those days you didn't really have time, you're at a racetrack every week and too busy getting ready, going racing then packing up and moving on. We didn't make a lot of money, it was always just enough to get you to the next racetrack and pay to take part in the meeting.

At the TT in '67 I also rode the Suzuki 250. It was just the once and it was something I didn't take too seriously. Harry Thompson wanted me to ride it in the production rice. He ran a business called Spa Motorcycles in Harrogate and quite a few guys rode his bikes at the TT. I have to confess I used that mainly to learn the track a bit more without having to use and wear out my own equipment. I didn't do all that well on it either, well I didn't think I did but I still finished 5th. Remarkably, the record books have me finishing twelfth on the Suzuki in the Lightweight race but I don't even remember taking part in that!

By the time the TT came around in 1968 I was getting very familiar with the course. I felt like I knew my way around by now. I was also the top privateer on the Aermacchi in the 350 class and I ended up third in the world championship. I was also the top privateer in the 125 class. I finished third in that race and that was one of my best ever results at the TT but I was behind Phil Read and Bill Ivy who did the 100mph lap, of course. I was miles ahead of the other guys who were on the regular production bikes. I felt I could have had a podium on the 350 in the Junior TT as well but of all the darned things, the tube on the front of the headstock on the bike that the rev counter was mounted on broke off and fell inside the fairing. I immediately slowed the bike down and made my way back to the pits to dig it out. The one thing you don't do at any track let alone the TT is go running around with a rev counter dangling next to the front wheel.

I was also on the Norton for a top 10 finish in the Senior race which was one of the weirdest I've been in. I should have finished second in the 500 class. The strange thing about it was I was getting signals saying I was either second or third over the opening couple of laps. So the race was going fine until halfway around lap three. I was blasting along at high speed and then suddenly the bike would just cut out. It would coast for a while and then come good again. When I got to the pits we changed the spark plug and away I went again. It was good for a lap and then this cutting out business began again so that's why I dropped from second back all the way to sixth. I eventually came tenth. I'm thinking '*what the hell is going on*'. Then I went to the Dutch TT and in practice I went out with hardly any fuel in the gas tank and it did exactly the same thing. I'm embarrassed to say I figured it out eventually. There was a breather pipe on the gas tank which was sticking out of the side of the fairing. However, it was only poking out by about an inch. When the tank was pretty full, there was no problem, the fuel would flow, yet when the tank was low, the air going past the end of this pipe put a vacuum in the gas tank and the fuel would stop running. That's why the damn thing kept quitting on me in the Isle of Man. All I did was pull the pipe out another three or four inches and that fixed it. It's quite an embarrassing story.

In 1969 Aermacchi gave me a 125, a 350 and a 380 for the 500 class. I was basically their factory rider. I went on to have some good results at the beginning of the season. When I got to the Isle of Man I did a 99 mile an hour lap on the 350. The next thing I know, the Benelli people came around asking if I'd like to ride their second bike. So I called the Aermacchi factory and they didn't have a problem with that because every year I just entered the 250 race even though I didn't have a bike, it was always just in case something came up and this time it did. So, I made a deal with Benelli that I'd ride the second bike. The idea was Phil Read was supposed to win the race. However, I was number one on the grid so off I went and at the end of the first lap, I was miles ahead of him and he was behind Rod Gould so I couldn't slow down. I then increased my lead but then started to slow down, waited for a bit and then I got a pit signal saying '1st, OK' so I just rumbled on and won the race.

Those pre-race agreements were part of the deal. I'd been in Europe for four years when I was offered a factory bike but then there are stipulations that go with it. We even went to the officials and tried to get Read to start number one and let me take his position. In fact, I believe number one on the grid in the Isle of Man isn't that good. You've no incentive, you don't see anybody a couple of hundred yards ahead of you, that sort of thing, who you're trying to catch. Actually, it was one of the easiest races

"They look at you and go,
'Christ, you won the Isle of
Man?' It's like they don't
get excited that I was world
champion more so the fact
that I won at the Isle of Man."

KEN CARRUTHERS

I've ever had in my life. It was also a great thrill for me, I must admit that.

I also finished as runner-up in the 125 race while in the 350 I was second behind Agostini on the last lap until I broke a rocker arm, which was very disappointing. After that, Benelli wanted to sign me as a backup rider for Renzo Pasolini, which I did. I then raced the rest of the season and Pasolini kept crashing which then meant I was given the good equipment he'd been getting. I then went on to win two of the last three races of the campaign, coming second in the other one, which meant I ended up winning the World title. It was pretty special. Strangely, winning the TT was almost more important than winning the championship. I've met people over the years and been introduced to them as '*Cal was 1969 World 250 champion. He also won the Isle of Man.*' They look at you and go, '*Christ, you won the Isle of Man?*' It's like they don't get excited that I was world champion more so the fact that I won at the Isle of Man.

We were still living in England at this time. I'd met a guy and he let us use his house which was near Brands Hatch. Other than that, we were on the road, this time with a bigger caravan than we'd been using and come winter we'd go back to Australia. In 1969 I was nominated for Australian Sportsman of the Year, however, unfortunately for me, this was the year Rod Laver dominated tennis around the world winning Wimbledon, the French, US and Australian opens. So I guess coming second wasn't such a bad result for me as far as that award was concerned. Plus, there was a big parade for me when I got home, in recognition of winning the championship.

1970 was to be my final year as a racer. I had a deal organised with Benelli to race the 350 but while I was home in Australia they got in touch to say they wouldn't be able to supply bikes because there was an industrial strike in Italy and that they only had equipment for Pasolini. So I needed to find a bike and back then Yamaha was the one to have but the only new 250 I could get my hands on was in America. I also found a year-old 350 at Don Vesco's in California. So I went to the States to collect the bikes and while I was there I rode one of Don Vesco's bikes at Daytona and won the 250 race. Before the race I told Don we needed to change the crankshaft but he disagreed. Anyway, halfway through the race the crankshaft went out halfway through. I think I'd have probably won the double had it stayed together. I went on to Europe and Renzo Pasolini had crashed again so Benelli offered me the bike for Opatija in Yugoslavia. I qualified fastest there but had gearbox trouble in the race and finished second to Ago. I also finished second to him at the Nurburgring and then we went to the Isle of Man where the chain fell off so I told them I'd had enough. They weren't paying me enough either so I chose to go back to my 350 Yamaha. Meanwhile, the 250 was having issues with contract breakers. If they didn't break then I would win the race. I knew I could have won all the races if I didn't have any problems. Eventually I got Krober ignition but it was kind of too late. The Isle of Man that year was another one of the easiest races I'd ever had. I started behind Santiago Herrero and Rodney Gould and I caught and passed them at the top of the mountain on the first lap so I knew then I could win this race as long as I didn't do anything stupid; I went on to win by two minutes or something. The track was dry but the surface began to deteriorate. It was really bad that year, the tar was melting. That was the race that Herrero was killed in. He crashed at the 13th milestone on the last lap and they said it was because of the melting tar. Stan Woods crashed trying to avoid him and broke an ankle and two collar bones. Herrero's team OSSA were so upset about it they abandoned racing altogether. In fact, I was the first rider to say anything bad about the TT. At the prize giving, the 250 had been the first race of the week and before we got our awards the likes of myself and Agostini had said we had to do something about this place. It was agreed that as I was the first one to get a trophy I'd be the first to say something. So I went up to get my trophy and made a speech about how proud I was to win the race, I was happy to be there but it was about time that the safety of the track was improved and then things just snowballed from there. More riders came on board with our way of thinking and eventually Ago said he'd had enough as did a lot of others.

Boy, did I get a reaction for what I'd said. I had the press all over me. It's an awful thing to say but the bike media back then seemed to love the fact people died there as it gave them a story. The motorcycle journalists hit back saying *'it's part of the racing, the challenge, it's traditional'* all that sort of stuff. I felt I came out of it fairly well, I was saying, *'I realise it's dangerous and you can't move houses or trees but you can put a lot more straw bales up plus you shouldn't have melted tar.'* I was soon forgotten about because the likes of Agostini and co became a lot more vocal and kind of carried the mantle and, of course, it lost its world championship. I still loved the event, I just wanted it to become a bit more safer.

There were some parts I didn't like. The worst bit was after you turned right at the Ballacraine hotel, it was horrible through there. It was bumpy with adverse camber. Another was after Braddan Bridge, that next section, pretty much all the way through. I didn't really have any favourite sections but the mountain was good. The way you raced the Isle of Man was to treat it as sections not corners. You're always thinking like three sweeps ahead..

The TT is weird because I would look forward to going there, I enjoyed it when I was there and I was relieved when it was over. It was always *'Thank God, that's done.'* Then, of course, you're looking forward to coming back next year.

Yet in all the time I raced there I never had any close calls.

At the end of 1970 MV Agusta wanted me to join Agostini but the powerful Italian journalists were clamouring for someone from Italy to be the second factory rider. Had I been offered that I would have stayed in Europe, instead I went to America for the following season, did a couple of years of racing there then I took over the engineering side of the team which then led me to taking Kenny Roberts to Europe. The first two years we did as the Yamaha America team and the third we were turned into the official factory team even though there was only myself and two mechanics plus Kenny. A little bit after that Ago came in with the Marlboro money so we moved the race team from Amsterdam down to Bergamo in Italy. I'd known him since 1966, not very well, but I knew him. We were working out of Ago's workshops and it went from there. We had Kenny and then Eddie Lawson on bikes I prepared and in ten years we won the 500cc World title six times.

As for my retirement as a racer, the first year I raced in the States I operated out of Don Vesco's shop and I prepared the bikes there. He had Dyno facilities and everything else I needed. My second year in America, I signed directly with Yamaha USA and part of my job was to teach Kenny Roberts road racing. The third year, Yamaha decided that they wanted to have a better organised race set-up so I took over. We formed the Yamaha America factory team, with Roberts, Gene Romero and Don Castro along with myself. I supplied the workshops and mechanics while Yamaha USA supplied the bikes, the riders and all the parts. So I was running the Yamaha team out of my workshops down in San Diego. I rode a few races, had some results like second at Daytona and I won Talladega. It just got to the stage where I was entered for a couple of races yet I just didn't have time to race, I was too busy looking after everything so it was pretty easy for me to quit racing because I had this full time deal with Yamaha. I was also doing development work for the Yamaha factory. I also had a relationship with Yamaha no other non-Japanese had ever had and probably never had since.

All through my career I did my own bikes. At the TT I would have had just a helper with me, just an extra pair of hands, not an engineer or anything. I was happy with that. The last year I was there, I had Nobby Clark helping me with the Yamaha. He was from Rhodesia and had been with Honda helping Mike Hailwood and Jim Redman earlier in the decade. Other than that at any other time, I just had a friend over there who was more or less on vacation. They'd take the wheels to Dunlop, jobs like that but I had nobody technical working with me.

There was a time when the TT organisers offered Kenny Roberts a heap of cash to race there. He came and sat down with my wife and I and we just told him not to do it. It was his first year in Europe. He'd never been to the TT and he didn't really like racing on regular roads. I said,

"*Kenny, you wouldn't know where you're going and you're going to get beaten by people that aren't as good as you plus, to be honest, it's kind of dangerous. You've got more important things to worry about.*"

I must say this for him, those first few years, both in America and in Europe, he took a lot of notice of what I was telling him. So he replied

"*okay then, I'm not going*",

which may not have been easy for him as they were offering a lot of money. At that time he was doing really well in the world championship and as far as he was concerned the TT was just another race. He'd never really thought about it and to be honest, it didn't take much effort to convince him that this wasn't a good idea.

Kenny and I had a good relationship. I looked after him and his bikes from the first time he rode the Yamahas in America until the day he retired.

I also got on well with Agostini when he was team boss at Marlboro. He was good. He let me run things the way I wanted to run them.

Since I retired I've been back to the Isle of Man something like three or four times and done a few parade laps. The first occasion was the year Benelli had the new three-cylinder Superbikes. They had the two prototype ones and I did a lap on that which I enjoyed. It ran at a reasonable speed and I could remember some of the track. The next time I went back I rode a 350 Yamaha and I'm going '*Jesus, how did we ever race these things around here?*' The Benelli was a big bike with suspension and big tyres, I felt comfortable on that but the Yamaha didn't feel so comfortable. The last time I was there I rode my 250 Benelli which was the actual bike I rode in the world championship. By then I realised '*Hell, I don't remember where I'm going.*' I didn't do anything fantastic as it was the parade lap.

When I think back I have some great TT memories. Winning the 250 race in 1969, my first TT victory. Winning it again the following year was another big deal for me. When I finished third in the 125 the year before that was probably the best race I ever had in the Isle of Man. My biggest disappointment was in '69 when the Aermacchi broke on the last lap in the Junior. I was miles in front of the third-placed guy.

I still hope to get back there again one day but it's expensive from the States. I'm in my eighties now but I'm in good health. I just saw the specialist for my yearly checkup and everything's good. Hopefully I'll be good for a long while. I'm a little guy who weighs something like 142lb. I don't drink, never smoked or done drugs in my life. So basically I'm in pretty good shape. I've just retired from working for the second time

One thing that's amazed many people is the fact the last motorcycle I owned was when I was 22 years of age. That was when I got married and we had a family early in life so you don't go running around on motorcycles when you have kids. To be honest, riding bikes on the street never really appealed to me that much. Where I used to live I'd ride a motocross bike around in the hills. I still watch the racing on television and I've been to the Grand Prix a couple of times in America. I enjoy it but there's some things about it that I don't like. I'm amazed the good guys fall off all the time! I've worked out that in the years I raced in Australia I crashed five times and on four or five occasions in Europe over the course of five years. Maybe I wasn't going fast enough!

At the TT, either in practice or the race, I've done a 99 mile-an-hour laps on three different bikes, but I never cracked 100. I never set out to do it. I can remember some riders who had people helping them, sorting out on sections to help them do a 100 mph lap yet I wasn't interested. I just went as fast as I wanted to go, as fast I felt I could go safely and it turned out to be an average speed of 99 miles an hour. It was how I made my living. You don't make any money if you're lying in a hospital all banged up.

The TT is very unique. It was important in my life because I always wanted to go there.

I never expected to win.

I was happy when I went there and I was more than happy when I won the damn thing.

Racing motorcycles is the best job I ever had and I was fortunate that when I finished racing, I had something that was just as important, to go straight to engineering with the race teams.

I raced motorcycles for 18 years, I never went to hospital and I never broke a bone.

I guess I was lucky.

Kel lives with his wife Jan in Marietta, which is about 65 miles north of San Diego, California. They had two children. His final season in Grand Prix was in 1995. The following year he worked for the factory Sea-Doo Watercraft team as an engineer and that was followed by AMA motocross with the Chaparral satellite Yamaha team. Then came retirement from sport but, having done woodwork as a hobby, he put his skills to good use for the next ten years, rebuilding vacated mobile homes for his son-in-law's family who ran a park. He's now retired ...unless, he says, something else comes along.

CAMERON DONALD

Born Melbourne, Australia

TT years 2006, 2008, 2010-16
2 x wins, 7 x 2nd, 1 x 3rd, 2 x4th, 3 x 5th, 1 x 6th, 2 x 7th, 1 x 9th, 3 x 10th, 2 x 11th, 4 x 13th, 1 x 16th, 1 x 18th, 15 x DNF

Classic TT years 2016-17
1 x 2nd, 1 x 4th, 1 x 12th, 1 x 16th, 1 x DNF

Cameron Donald's impact on the TT was almost immediate, bagging a brace of wins in only his third year of competition. Hailing from Australia, the Isle of Man was never on the radar despite him being the son of a TT fan but all that changed when he won the Supersport class at the Macau Grand Prix which eventually led him on a journey to the Mountain course. His first year at the Island was on a 600 yet when he returned to ride a 1000cc Superbike for the first time he was on record breaking pace. A successful TT career ensued with a string of impressive results and performances over a ten year period.

My grandfather had a motorbike and sidecar as transport so I come from a motorcycling family. As my dad was an only child that's how they travelled back in those days, it was simply because it was all they could afford. So my Pop would ride his motorbike to work and on the weekend, if it was a family trip out, they'd bolt the sidecar on. My dad was always mad keen on bikes even though he was a truck mechanic and had motorcycles from a young age including an AJS Matchless 350 that he commuted on, as well as using for club racing. He only did a little bit of competing, as times were tough. He'd service someone's truck for free and in return would borrow it for the weekend so he could go racing; just put his bike on the back and take it to the races. Dad lived and breathed bikes plus it was always British machinery. As I was growing up he always talked about the TT, especially Manx Nortons, in fact, any bike or rider that had done something at the Isle of Man. He was always talking about the Island, especially with my great uncle. So as I listened to them it was always on my mind too.

I started racing quite late in life. Like dad, my older brothers had raced Junior motocross. They're a bit older than me but when they became teenagers they lost interest and dropped out right about the time that I started saying '*Dad, I want to race*'. He was like '*no, we've been down this road, it costs too much.*' and did everything he could to persuade me not to do it. That was until I dropped out of school at 15 and got a job at a local bike shop, which I did because I wanted to start racing. It was then dad realised '*okay, this is serious.*' So I started competing at 15 on dirt tracks and then onto the bitumen circuit racing. I hadn't really thought much about racing at the TT until I had the opportunity to go to Macau and fill in for an injured rider. That was my first street race and I ended up winning the Supersport class in my debut at the Macau Grand Prix. I was on the same track as the likes of Michael Rutter, Dave Jefferies, John McGuinness and I knew these guys from the TT having watched them in videos back home. So that was my first street race and my introduction to a TT-type meeting. I then came over to the UK to do a couple of rounds of BSB for Northern Irish team Barron Transportation Racing at Mondello and Thruxton on ex-AIM Suzukis. Billy Barron, the BTS team owner, asked if I fancied flying from Northern Ireland on a little charter plane to check out the Isle of Man Senior TT with them. The crazy thing is I didn't even know what date the TT was on. That sounds ignorant but it's just not knowing about such things being on the other side of the world. I would have read about it in Australian Motorcycle News, probably a month after it had happened. I'd always be interested in it, always look at the photos, any on-boards and be like, '*Wow!*' So I'm over in Northern Ireland, and the guys are like '*TT is on, we're going over for Senior day*' and I'm like '*what? The TT is on now?*' And they're like '*Yeah.*' So we flew over and the boys took me down to Ballagarey; that was the first corner where I watched from. One of the first riders I saw go through was Bruce Anstey who, ironically, would later become my teammate. Literally, as the first bikes came through, I just looked at the boys and said, '*I'm going to come and do this. I'm going to try it.*' I came home, told my folks and in fact anyone I knew '*I'm just gonna go and do it once, just want to tick the box.*' And the rest is history.

On that first visit to the Isle of Man I went up to the race paddock and found TT supremo Paul Phillips to basically tell him '*this is who I am. I've raced a heap of short circuits and I've won Macau's supersport class. I want to do the TT, if you hear of anyone that's got a spare bike. Let me know.*' Paul eventually got back to me to tell me that Gordon Blackley, who rode for some mechanics for the RAF was due to race at the TT but couldn't anymore. I was put in touch with Mick Charnock, who ran TC Racing with a couple of the RAF guys. The deal was they would sponsor my bike, while I would pay for the fuel and the consumables. I'm not trying to make it out like a hard luck story but we had no money. They still had a big shock when I turned up with my suitcase which had a spare chain, gearing, and a couple of sets of brake pads in it. I'd brought all my consumables with me because I worked in a bike shop at home so therefore I could get them cheaper. The guys will back me up on that story. I was just begging them to please let me run the bike on pump fuel, not ELF because I found out how much it was a litre. At the time, the Aussie dollar was like 2.7 or something to one pound. It was around $8 a litre for fuel back then so they let me run it on pump fuel which was the best thing I ever did.

No-one will do what I did back then because everyone wants to ride every class. Just concentrating on the Supersport category was the best way forward because it gave me the opportunity to do nothing but focus on the track. In my opinion, the best way to learn the TT circuit is on a smaller capacity machine which means it's more about finding that flowing line instead of trying to control a bike that wants to spit you off. On the 1000 you're just gritting your teeth and hanging on to the thing so I really focused on the 600 plus we did great. Then of course that was when you could still run a 600 in the Senior and there was a couple of thousand quid on offer for the top Supersport finisher so that was in my head because I was so skint. I remember riding around thinking '*Holy shit, I can win two grand*' but that thought went straight out of my head when the thing threw a rod during the race. So we didn't finish the Senior but being on the 600 was still a brilliant way to learn the track plus I had really good mechanics that had total faith and trust in me along with a pretty reasonable standard 600. There's no doubt in my mind, that was the perfect way to do it.

Before then the only time I'd seen footage of the TT was back in Australia, when we would get the Duke videos, the on-board ones. This of course was pre-internet, pre-YouTube and being able to look up anything you want online as you can these days and the first on-board video I ever owned was a rider on a CBR 600. I watched it a bunch of times, it made a huge impression on me and I was like '*wow, that's crazy*' but not once did I ever think about racing it; at the time it never even crossed my mind. I just wanted to go racing Superbikes on purpose-built tracks, that was always my goal because with no street racing in Australia it just didn't really seem an option to go to the other side of the world. The TT was never really on my radar but in saying that I lived in the hills and that played a part in my racing destiny. I got my licence when I was young. I always loved riding on the road so I really enjoyed riding on the street. When I went to Macau, I really got a buzz doing a street race. It was so crazy. That's when I started thinking about the Isle of Man. I was like, '*okay, street race, that's a buzz.*' Then I started watching a few more on-board videos and I'm thinking, '*well, jeez, I'm as fast as some of these guys.*' It started to become real having seen it for myself from the hedge. I want to go there and just finish. Once I saw this circuit with my own eyes, breathed it in, then all it was about for me was just riding it and getting a finishing medallion. That was my goal. I just wanted to finish in the medals. Having watched from Ballagarey earlier that day we went to the Villa Marina at night-time for the awards ceremony after the Senior and as the trophy is being handed out I'm thinking '*I want a medal.*' So that was really the motivation. I didn't know any of the riders but later that year I spoke to some of them at Macau when I went back for a second time. A couple gave me a bit of advice like, just learn the circuit in sections and break it down, don't overthink it, just get an idea of what direction it went.

When I went to the TT in 2004 as a spectator I was also racing in the Asian Pacific championship, which is a 600 Supersport series but I was on a mission to try to get to World SuperSport and even British Supersport. I spoke to Jack Valentine at Valmoto after getting good results at the TT and they were really keen, so they started throwing some figures around but I was just like, '*can't do it, that's out of my price league.*'

So I came over to the TT to prepare, I was bloody fit as well because I was racing all the time and I still had quite a few years under my belt, I wasn't a kid anymore, I felt prepared. I was racing at a professional level, high-speed 600 Supersport. The Asian championship was insane. It was more competitive than anyone probably gave it credit for. WIth the TT on the horizon all I did was watch a heap of on-board laps, especially the CBR600 one. I just watched that over and over again. Another piece of advice I can give to newcomers is don't study a fast lap. Don't get a Hickman or Dunlop 135 mph an hour, you miss too much detail. Get a slower lap, get 120 mile an hour lap, take in all the details. So I just watched it, watched it, watched it and to be honest, I'd watched it so many times that when I came over I really felt as if I knew the place. I got there a couple of days before practice started, borrowed a car and went out around the course. I tried to do four laps, two in the morning, two in the afternoon, when the traffic had died down. That first time I came over as a spectator with the boys we didn't even do a complete lap. We only drove sections of it and took shortcuts. So before I came out for my first race, I hadn't done a complete lap. I'd really applied myself to learning the circuit via the on-boards. That first lap I rode on a bike was mind blowing, totally awesome. I've got a photo somewhere of when I came back to the pits straight after my very first session. I had a grin just like a split watermelon. It was such a buzz. I wasn't daunted by the lack of run-off. I wasn't scared, I was just excited. That was just pure adrenaline. I felt very comfortable on the CBR 600. I'd raced one in Asia so I knew the bikes. I was loving every minute of it. I just wanted to do more laps because I could see, with each one, it was just coming to me. I can't remember the first night whether I did two or three but I remember it was interesting because Les Shand, the Scottish rider, was a newcomer as well, he was next to me waiting to go out and as I looked over at him he had this look on his face of just total stress. I see that now with newcomers and I'm just like, '*oh man, what a terrible way to start your TT career.*' Me, I was just beaming. It was the best thing I'd ever done on a motorbike, without a doubt and I'd done some pretty cool stuff.

One of the boys in my team, the RAF guys, they were such a good crew but they're like '*hmmm, Les doesn't look too happy.*' We were both on the newcomers bus and we signed our newcomers briefing together. I'd met him in Macau, so we were just sort of chatting a bit yet he was frightened before it had even started but he went on to do very well as a newcomer. I just clicked with it and just loved it. Every single session, I went out, getting quicker each night. I kept telling the guys I don't have to ride any harder than I am doing. I'm just gaining circuit knowledge. Then it gets to the point where, all of a sudden, you're not going a mile any quicker every lap so you really have to start applying yourself to keep moving forward.

My dad was thrilled that I was doing it. I was ticking the box. He was used to me being away racing in Asia and far from home. I always travelled on my own or with a mechanic, a guy called Rod, he was pretty renowned in Australia. He'd raced in European and worked for Yamaha Netherlands. He was spannering for Kim Newcombe, the Kiwi rider, who was leading the World championship on that bike with the outboard motor from West Germany, the Konig. Rod had known and lost friends at the TT over the years so he wasn't really keen on me doing it but we made a deal. He said,

"do it once I'll help you but we just do it once,"

to which I agreed. Rod was the guy that got me over to Asia from Australia and spannered for me there. He really helped me through it in lots of ways. It's interesting because since I went back to the TT our friendship's never really been the same since. He'll always be like a dad to me but I think he took it pretty hard that I kept coming back; it was just because he worried about me.

When I rode in the Senior TT the best thing that could have happened was the 600 throwing a rod going into Signpost. Up until then everything I touched turned to gold but this taught me how quick this place could bite you. That was a good way to cap the year off. It sent me home thinking a bit more seriously than I would have been had it not happened. I thought, if I apply myself to this place then I can get a result in three years. Everyone was saying one year to work out which way it goes, second year to build some speed, third year to go for a result so that was in the back of my head. I'll give it three years and reckon I can get a result. I was no longer thinking of just getting a finish and never coming back again. The TT bug had bitten me. I was trying to get to racing in Europe, I had an opportunity to go do some Dutch Supersport which, hopefully, was going to lead to World Supersport but I was getting screwed around and being asked for money. After that first year when I came home to Australia I was still short circuit racing, but everything I was doing, I was thinking about the TT, everything was about TT, my training, I was thinking about the TT. Everything I did was so focused on going back and riding that track faster and faster.

Then right about that time Uel Duncan, who had his own race team in Northern Ireland called and said

"Look, do you want to go road racing?"

I'd been burned so many times trying to negotiate a deal from Australia and Europe so I replied *"yep, what the hell! Let's go."*

I'd also had an invite from the DMR Honda team in Northern Ireland to race at the Ulster Grand Prix, which I'd accepted. I solely did that to get myself back to Europe, still trying to get a Supersport ride. That's the only reason I did this because they covered my airfare plus gave me a couple of quid. So I went to the Ulster, won the Newcomers race and grabbed a podium in a wet Supersport race. I did really well. That started making me think the roads were fun plus it was less bullshit. The people involved were genuine. I loved the vibes so when Uel Duncan called I just went

"you know what, stuff the circuits.' For now. I'm gonna go and race the TT"

and that led me to riding for Uel.

They were really good bikes. I had an ex-Karl Harris Honda and Eugene Laverty's CBR 600. Plus an ex-Karl Harris 1000. They bought four bikes, two 600s and two 1000s for myself and Les Shand. I was on the other side of the world, I'd just come over with my girlfriend at the time. We never had any family or any other support. We literally had no money. I had to pay for fuel and tyres. So I was doing that by basically winning prize money at the National road circuits. Other sponsors soon came on board and helped with the odd set of tyres or drum of fuel. Gareth Robinson of Robinsons concrete, Wilson Craig and Uel Duncan, the three of them together were amazing at what they did for me. I was young, unbelievably motivated, at the time I was fully trying to go to the World Supersport Championship and thinking I was good enough for a 600 ride there. So my level was high and I was full of anger, what I mean by that is I felt I had a point to prove. I'd been screwed around before and that showed in the National road races in Northern Ireland that year. Uel mentored me a lot. I had so much belief in everything he told me. A perfect example of that is when I asked him

"How do you take Bray Hill on the Superbike?"

and he just said

'well, flat-out!'"

I later went on a chat show in the Isle of Man with John McGuinness and Ryan Farquhar plus a few others and someone asked

"*How do you go through Bray Hill?*"

One said if you have a couple of days of rubber down, if everything's working just right, you can get through flat-out on a Superbike and someone else's like

"*you get through flat on maybe four laps out of the six.*" I remember looking at them, then looking at Uel thinking, *'I just hold it flat every single lap!'* I kid you not but I did. The thing could be tying itself in a knot yet I was just *'well, Uel said I could do it'* and I believed him.

I was pretty fast in that first year in 2006 on a Superbike. I ended up second in the Senior to John McGuinness with a best average lap of 128 and a half miles an hour. I set a new lap record and then moments later John pipped it. When I look back to that day, I regard that personally as my greatest achievement at the TT.

In hindsight, the bike was an angry beast to ride. It was a BSB machine, it didn't even have a starter motor. We bump started every pit-stop. Everyone involved was just doing their best, some beautiful people, it was like being in a family, they took in myself and my girlfriend from Australia. That meant I had less distractions, I was there to do a job and keep everything else out of my focus really, just there to ride the bike. I was a relative newcomer but I still had fantastic machinery plus support and I just clicked. When I came home to Australia I was still short circuit racing, but everything I was doing, I was thinking about the TT, everything was TT, in training, I was thinking about the TT. Everything I did was so focused on going back and riding that track faster and faster.

I had quite a bit of interest from several teams after what happened in 2006 yet I wouldn't even answer their calls. I wasn't interested because Uel had given me that chance, so there was no way I was going anywhere. I was more than confident of winning with the team. So we sort of geared up to do a second year and then I got hurt at the North West 200 in Northern Ireland. That was the first year my dad came over. My mom did too. They'd been separated since I was three or four but they came over, mom with her husband plus other friends travelling through Europe on their way to the TT. Dad ended up coming anyway and stayed when I got hurt. We went over to the Isle of Man to watch together which was kind of cool because I got to sit on the hedge and have a pint with him. He probably enjoyed it more without me riding.

My mom never made it over to the TT and never has but she did see me in Northern Ireland. When I got hurt that was hugely devastating. I ended up speaking to Philip Neill at TAS Racing who'd shown an interest in me and I could see how the professional teams were doing things a little bit differently plus, I was quite keen to get into the British championship as I could see that I could be better off there. Uel and the guys were more than happy to take me to a couple of rounds of the British but for them, it was more to keep me happy, it wasn't really what they wanted to do. So, at the end of 2007, I knew it was time to make a move and I signed to ride for the Relentless Suzuki by TAS Racing team.

Without doubt finishing second on the Superbike was my greatest achievement but that first TT win in 2008 was the best result of my racing life. Just to stand atop the TT podium was incredible. I remember it like it was yesterday. I can recall everything about it. Standing on the podium, looking at the Australian flag flying on the back of the grandstand and thinking about what I'd just done. I spoke with my dad about that afterwards. He used to hop on his 350 AJS to go to work as a diesel mechanic and ride from Warrendyke, up a twisting sort of mountain road out of town yet he used to pretend he was racing up the Mountain Mile at the TT. He'd never been there. Never, ever thought he would get there but he'd read about it. So for me to not only race there but win it well, you could see how much it meant to him. So he shared in this amazing, amazing feeling. Any result you get at the TT, they never come in easy. It's just excitement, it's relief.

At the time, I was just so confident and on a roll. I was just like, '*bring on the next race.*'

I really wanted that next win so bad. You can win one with a bit of luck and John McGuinness had a DNF in that race, so that went in my favour.

"Without doubt finishing second on the Superbike was my greatest achievement but that first TT win in 2008 was the best result of my racing life."

CAMERON DONALD

It was really tough conditions in that superstock race, but yeah, it felt good. My focus was on the big bikes. I never really gelled with the Suzuki 600 and I don't think I ever had quite the same bike as Bruce Anstey had. That was fine though; it was not really my goal. Then of course, there was the Senior and what could have been, but things were looking good.

Philip Neill helped me greatly. He is a great mentor and a great friend. I remember him saying that I couldn't get away with riding like this all the time, save it for when there's a win on the table. In one race at the North West 200, while I was still racing for Uel Duncan, I had to start from the back of the back of the grid. I eventually got through to whatever position, fourth or fifth, before crashing and smashing my collarbone in 2007. One of the other riders came up to me on the grid before the start of that race and said,

"You can't do anything from here, just finish."

I didn't even look at him. I just stared straight ahead, blanking him and I remember inside my helmet thinking *'yeah, watch me,'* even though he was saying it as a friend.

I was so motivated, definitely not full of myself but I had plenty of self-confidence, self-belief and that's how I was riding at the TT. I wasn't scared of dying, that's for sure. I know it sounds terrible and it's no secret, I've told people this before but I used to look at myself in the mirror, maybe having just had a shower in the morning before going down to the track and I used to actually say to myself,

"Well, today's as good a day to die as any other, let's get this on."

I look back at that attitude now and I just cringe but I was young, I was riding well plus I was superfit. I had good bikes. Everything was there even though I'd had injuries and I knew the sport could bite you hard.

I was still thrilled to finish second in the Senior TT in 2008. It's the same race as the first Superbike to a point. Of course, I would have loved to win the Senior, that would have been brilliant but at the time I went '*well, I know I can beat John.*' I didn't win because I'd had a mechanical. My attitude was *'I'll just win next year.'* That's why I took the disappointment of not winning so well because I was just thrilled as the bike was on its last legs. I was ecstatic that I finished the race, got the Joey Dunlop trophy for scoring the most points, got the extra 10 grand so brought home some extra prize money for finishing the race because I could have just as easily been parked up on the side of the road. I was just thrilled I got home in second place and took the overall trophy.

I stayed with TAS for another year as Suzuki moved onto a new bike, the K9 and it was massive. It was so different to what they'd produced before and like all manufacturers that get a new model and come to the TT, they tend to struggle. Remember the first year of the BMW? They struggled, the first year of the new Kawasaki, they struggled. That's why Honda keeps going good because they've got a great base set-up from the word go. It doesn't matter how many nights of practice there are, the bike is already in the ballpark. The Suzuki at that stage was a completely new bike and we struggled with it. We found out why later, there was different tyre construction and we'd gone totally the wrong way with the chassis set-up, making it too rigid but we didn't learn this. Everything was late arriving so we didn't test enough. We struggled at the North West and a bit of that was put back on me, with some folk suggesting '*you've won one, gone home and sat on your laurels.*' That wasn't the case. Nothing comes easy. No-one realised how hard my off-season was when I went home. I was happy but I had never, ever trained as hard as I did then. I was on a mission to come back fitter and stronger, I was thinking '*you wait and see what I've been doing,*' I was so motivated, However, I just didn't click with that bike.

We struggled all the way through TT practice week, having a hell of a time. Myself and Bruce were off the pace until the second last night of practice when the guys in the team decided to put us on the K8, which was the previous year's bike, '*just to give us some direction.*' That was solely why. There was no way we could race this new machine yet we couldn't pass it with Suzuki. The plan was to do a lap on the K8, come in and say '*it does this, where the new bike doesn't do that,*' we were so lost at this point. As I was rolling out of the pits, Lee Finlay, my mechanic leaned over and said to me, '*Hey, I filled the tank, if it feels good, stay out and do two laps.*'

I was two miles in and I was like, *'Oh my god, this is so much better'*. I didn't even know how fast I was going, I just thought *'oh, I'm back on the bike that I should be on.'* Everything clicked. As I came out of the Nook, I looked down at the dash. And I was like *'holy shit. This is a really fast lap.'* I remember thinking *'I'm not even trying.'* So I put my head down thinking about the next lap and did 131 mph, it was the first lap at that speed, a new unofficial lap record. I came in later and told the team

"I can go a lot faster than that or you can put me back on the other bike. It's up to you. I can ride the K9 and we might finish top five or put me on the old bike, the K8 and I will win the Superbike as well as the Senior."

Philip responded with

"we'll make it happen."

On the next night, the final practice session, there were spots of rain. Therefore, I wasn't going out. So I'm mentally prepared not to go out and at the last minute, someone, I can't remember who, suggested I just do a lap on the Superstock bike, which was the K9, to bed in brake-pads and stretch the chain for the race. I chased Conor Cummins out and I was actually sticking with him for quite a while even though he was on the Superbike. I was just having fun because I was so full of confidence and couldn't wait to get back on the K8 for the Superbike race on the following day. Coming down the mountain, I'd let Conor go by that stage so he'd pulled away, therefore I was just riding along not really pushing, which is always when you make mistakes. Going into Keppel Gate I missed a gear and the rest is history.

I remember it like it was yesterday. I was down changing when I missed the gear, I went into the turn a bit wide when I let the clutch out so I was half committed and there were still damp patches on the road. I was going off the racing line and as I'm running wide I remember thinking *'Oh fuck, fuck'*. I then looked up and they've actually widened the verge now, had it been like that then I probably could have made it but I looked at the grass and thought *'just go for that, play it safe'* because I didn't want to get hurt before racing. So I hit the brakes as hard as I could, then let the brakes off and the moment I hit the grass I remember just thinking '*fuck, I'm going heaps faster than I thought I was*'. I'd never spectated there or walked around, I didn't realise there's bloody holes in the grass everywhere. Riding past it looks like turf but within a couple of metres of being on the grass I found out to my cost it wasn't the surface I expected. As soon as I found a hole I was flicked over the bars and next thing I'm lying in a heap thinking about how my shoulder's now behind my back and that I've just stuffed it.

There were two guys spectating and both ran straight up to me. One of them is saying

"*Are you okay, are you okay?*"

while the other one's going

"*fuck, look at his arm*".

My shoulder was dislocated, my arm was up my back. I remember just thinking '*oh no*' but literally within minutes, the chopper was on the ground. The medics were just amazing and I felt so safe. The pain in my shoulder, which is the worst I've ever had, was still nothing compared to missing the race. Philip and the TAS guys were at the hospital, they were worried about me, but I really just thought '*well, we'll just make up for it next year.*' I thought I'm only going to get faster.

For sure, the injury hit home. A lot changed in my life around that time too. I guess, when I look back, I have spent a lot of time trying to break down what happened. As you grow older, your thinking becomes a little bit more mortal. It was a big injury. That was a fracture dislocation, it was quite complex and it didn't heal. It took me a long time to get over that which included a lot of rehab in Northern Ireland with doctors telling me this and that and all the while I was still trying to ride but not reaching my previous heights. I'm certain the guys around me thought I'd just lost my bottle which didn't help. We were like family so it wasn't difficult to see what they were thinking. I could see it in their eyes, people were questioning whether I could still do it. I'd had bad injuries before so I knew I could come back from it. I was seeing a specialist, having had a decent operation on the shoulder. It was just taking quite a long time to get over. When I did I felt I was not only a safer rider but a better one too. The problem was I just didn't click with the new Suzuki after that but was I the only one not to? Did it ever get a result at the TT after that? I don't think so even though I came close when I ran off at the Nook in the Superbike TT in 2010, did a u-turn and came back on the track. I'd lost a huge amount of time which I'm sure cost me the race. I still worked hard to work my way onto the podium. There was no question in my mind that I was going to win more TT races, I just needed to be on the right bike.

It was tough leaving TAS Racing and Suzuki because we'd been very close, like brothers almost, the mechanics plus team bosses Hector and Phillip Neill. I'd lived in Northern Ireland for some time, however a lot of things weren't working out for me. We ended the year at Macau where I was leading the race until it was stopped, which was tough to take as I believe I'd have won if we'd kept going because after the restart the bike overheated and blew a fuse. To me, it proved I was still riding well but I thought, if they're not going to change the tyres, the suspension or whatever else, which is what I was hoping they'd do, then what's going to change with the results? Everyone else seemed to be moving forward while I just didn't have confidence in the bike plus I could see what the others were winning on. I was also frustrated with the 600. I came from a Supersport background yet constantly hearing that it wasn't a strong class for me. That's one of the reasons I signed for Wilson Craig in 2011 as he ran very competitive 600 machines. It was a class that no-one seemed to fancy me in and while we didn't win any TT races we came very close more than once. I was leading a restarted one when the motor went pop because it had done two laps more than it should have. There would be several 600cc podium finishes including one of the closest in TT history when I was pipped by Bruce Anstey. There were good results too on the Superbike. I felt I'd made the right choice by switching to Honda.

You need to have faith in your bike. The Senior TT in 2008 is a case in point and was some race. In my heart of hearts I knew I was on fire in that one. No matter how hard John McGuinness pushed, I felt I pushed harder. I believed if I didn't win then I wouldn't cross the finish line.

Where I was within myself in terms of faith in my own ability at that time, I would never get back to that, it was before my big crash but it wasn't the accident that was the reason, it was just being on that bike. That K8 Superbike was a monster that I clicked with; I could do things with it that I couldn't with any other bike and it was the same with the 600 Honda. When you really gel with a bike, and that's where I was, it's a beautiful place to be. I'd gapped John before the bloody thing started leaking oil. I'd started pulling away with something like plus two seconds or whatever it was. When I got the next pit board the lead was getting bigger and I'm like '*you're on*'. I felt like a boxer, I had him on the ropes. I had him on the ropes and I was really going to give it to him. That is what was going on in my head until what happened happened and then I was like, '*Ah, shit.*' It was a beautiful race though.

When you're racing, and I had similar battles with Bruce Anstey, when you are neck and neck and you're pushing then see a board that says '*P1 plus nothing*' then the next one is '*P2 minus nothing*' then suddenly, you're going into corners at speeds you always wondered whether you could take them in. You manage it but by the next board your rival is still there and you're like, '*what am I gonna have to do?*' That's the thing about the TT because you can't see the other riders. Half the time you don't even know who it is you're up against until you arrive at your pitstop. Whether it was John or Bruce and they're on a different brand of bike or a different brand of tyre and you think '*how are you doing what I'm doing*?' So you're fighting these individual little battles. It's just you and your bike against this circuit. You're against this other rider that you're just learning about on the lap-board. It's the TT. I had other opportunities elsewhere but for me, at the TT, the Honda is a known quantity. We had our shortcomings in that first year with Wilson, we did have some podiums so it was like, '*Okay, let's build on this then come back.*' I knew the Superbike was our weak point. Being a privateer team, there were a lot of shortfalls. They didn't have full-time people or a full-time workshop, bikes were being prepared here and there. So the plan for the second year was to come back stronger yet we didn't. We were nowhere near as well prepared or as strong as the first year. Our results showed that and so I was going to bail. I was quite keen to go and ride for Clive Padgett. However, I'd done two years and perhaps learned from the mistakes but ultimately we hadn't. I felt I was riding the bike well enough each year, it just seemed like the package wasn't there. I'm not blaming the machine it's just the preparation wasn't there, the testing wasn't there and I probably shot myself in the foot. I probably should have just moved to the UK after 2009 because everything was being done on the phone. I missed home a lot so I would leave Australia as late as I could. I thought I could miss testing opportunities so when I turned up the bikes weren't even built; this wasn't what I'd believed over the previous six weeks. I suppose if I had been at the workshop and talking to people then maybe things would have been different so I've only got myself to blame for that.

At this point I felt I'd had enough plus I was now with my partner Kaz who was expecting our child. She didn't really want to start a family yet I wanted to have a kid just so I didn't have to race the TT. I had this feeling deep down that I wasn't going to the TT to finish second; the reason I went there was to win. I knew how hard I was pushing plus at the TT you started to lose friends. You would get to know people, think '*yeah, he's a nice guy*' but then something would happen to them which was sad but at the same time you'd think '*well, it wasn't me*' so move on. The more it happens the more it starts to eat away at you and you start thinking '*well hang on, maybe this is a numbers game*'. So Kaz is pregnant and I'm like, '*sweet, We're going to start a family therefore I won't race.*' Then Mick Grant called to see if I'd be interested in riding the Norton. At first I was like '*No, not really.*' but he came back with '*It'll probably pay well, you could maybe name a figure,*' which wasn't quite the case.

With Mick involved it got me thinking so I rang Steve Plater who was also involved in the project and he's like, '*everything's ready to go down Bray Hill.*' Since then I've joked it was ready to go down there in the back of the van, not with me sitting on it but I knew they would look after us, pay us well plus I could bring the whole family over. I asked Kaz how she felt and she was behind me so I decided to do it. So there we were with a five-week-old child, jumped on the plane and headed over to do a couple of years more racing. There was no pressure to get a result riding for Norton. As dad rode pommy bikes for me to ride for the factory Norton team was huge. Everyone was excited. I wasn't thinking about getting a result, I was just thrilled about the prospect of being heavily involved in developing a bike from the ground up. Mick was talking at the time of having my input to design chassis and do this and do that. Of course, we all know now that we, including Mick, were all being led down a path and that it was pretty much all smoke and mirrors from the Norton factory owner. At the time, I thought I was going to be involved in something fantastic so I headed over there. However, the first year was a disaster, the second was better because we had horsepower but a bike that didn't handle. To be fair, it was an amazing adventure but, as far as I was concerned, the bike was just a deathtrap. The whole thing was sad, because everyone including the young guys involved, they all wanted it. However, every time I had meetings with Norton owner Stuart Garner, I would tell him

"*We need grey hair in this pit. We need experienced mechanics, you can't go to the TT with a bunch of fresh graduates.*"

They wanted it to work as badly as anyone but the problem was experienced mechanics cost money who would then have told Norton what they didn't want to hear. For the third season, I was gonna get three times as much money as the year before yet I walked away because I thought this bike's gonna kill me. I still felt fit. I was riding well, I was pushing the Norton as hard as any other bike I rode. Meanwhile, Wilson Craig was always asking me to come back. I thought, you know what, I know I can still get a result so why not go back on the Honda. Deep down I thought it'd probably be my last year before I take a year out anyway. I was training very hard plus I was still racing in Asia and riding very fast. So I came back to the TT on the Honda and we had three engine failures in practice week. That was the moment I knew enough was enough. I was done.

The Superbike fired a rod during practice near McGuinness's; there was no warning, Bang! Threw a rod, oil everywhere, clutch in, back tyre brushed the hedge. It was a huge hit. I don't know how I stayed on it. I rolled up to this beautiful country house on the left there, a big white building, and a beautiful manicured garden. I rolled the bike down the front yard and lent it against a tree. I got off, looked at the machine and there was oil everywhere due to the hole in the side of the crankcase. I lay down and looking at the sky I thought about Kaz plus I thought about our daughter Lola and I was *'you know what, I didn't sign up for this. I'm done.'* I didn't tell anyone except Kaz that night in bed. I'd decided I wasn't even gonna race, told the guys but they were insistent I had to race. I was even more insistent that I wasn't!

"I've had three engine blow-ups, I'm fucking done!"

Two of them were catastrophic. I started the first Superbike race, got to the bottom of Bray Hill, turned left and that was the last race I did at the TT on a modern bike. It was a sad way to finish and it broke my heart. However, I couldn't race for a result so what was the point? I knew I was capable of getting a result but to do it, I needed to move back to the UK, do other races and spend time there. I'd started a young family and I had my block of land at home. I just wanted to build a house and start a new life.

I was showing an interest in doing more media work at the time. It's something that always interests me. I loved it. I felt I had a lot to bring. I can't remember who I spoke to but I'd let Paul Phillips know I was keen. Thankfully, North One got in touch, they were covering the TT TV broadcasts at the time and James Whitham, who worked for them as a commentator was unwell so they asked if I could come in to be part of the team. It was an opportunity for me. James is a hell of a nice guy plus he is a hero of mine. I sent him a message, I didn't know how he was and how it was going but I just said,

"Hey, mate, I've been offered this opportunity"

and he was like,

"*mate go for it, it's not something I'm going to do at the moment.*"

So I had that opportunity which I grabbed with both hands. It led to heaps of other stuff for me, not just that media opportunity but my TT racing has enabled me to do media work back here in Australia and in

Asia. The more media stuff you do the more comfortable you get, the more you learn. I approached it a bit like racing the TT, prepare, prepare, prepare and learn, learn and learn. The TT in Australia is huge. The percentage of visitors from Down Under is big now. We have a lot of people coming over and not just for the first time many are return travellers. I know this as I work for a company called SportsNet as a tour ambassador. The last year before it was cancelled due to Covid we had 265 people just on the premium tour. They charter a jet from Manchester just for those clients. It's huge in Australia and it's becoming big in Asia too. I've worked on the MotoGP coverage for the Fox channel out there and that's because I'm known as a TT racer. It's getting bigger and bigger around the world. It was just a perfect fit for me and I was very lucky to get the opportunity.

Had I not then maybe I would have turned into a bloody reclusive alcoholic or something. Giving up the TT when you're still fit and able to race or for whatever reason is bloody hard to do especially as I love the Isle of Man. I've got friends who are like family and I miss their company all year round. So I've always wanted to come back but I don't know if I could have returned and sat on the hedge without having a reason. The TV work gives me a reason. It's kept me relevant. It gives me an excuse to be in the paddock. It's been the ultimate way of weaning myself off racing.

There's the Aussie fans at the TT as well that gives me purpose. I help them with spectator areas along with the bus tours every year. I'll organise riders to join me on the coach. It's brilliant. I've had the likes of Steve Plater and Bruce Anstey on board, current and past riders, the list goes on and on. There's a big gala dinner with a chat show and there are guests for that too, John McGuinness, Ian Hutchinson and James Hillier to name a few. For the fans from Australia it's like this Holy Grail. '*One day, we'll get there*,' but from Australia it always seems difficult yet companies like SportsNet make it achievable. The ones who come, a lot of them are in their 50s, 60s and 70s. They've grown up idolising the TT, knowing all about the riders and bikes but never thought they'd ever get there. Then they're sitting at dinner with John McGuinness, Bruce Anstey and Ian Hutchinson. It's a pleasure for me to help put this together, there's a great amount of satisfaction that I get out of it. It may not be the same as flat out down Bray Hill but helping people tick boxes is a very special feeling.

Cameron lives with his partner Kaz and two girls in Warrendyke, a little village just outside of Melbourne in a house they built on his grandfather's block of land where the Donald family grew up. The family are bike mad, Cameron's daughter has just started taking part in competitive trials, while Kaz has partnered him in classic sidecar events. He's commentated on MotoGP for Fox Asia as well as work for magazines and websites. Away from racing he works in construction, which is something he's done for many years.

DAVID HICKMAN

Born Burton upon Trent, England

TT Years 1978
1 race, 1 x 31st

MGP Years 1976-77
3 races, 1 x win, 1 x 10th, 1 x DNF

David Hickman is one of the rare breeds who was just as good with a set of spanners as he was riding a bike. A promising career cut short by a life-changing injury but that didn't stop him using his skills to help others in their pursuit of success. A British champion and Manx Grand Prix winner he played a big part in revitalising the Norton brand in the late '80s and helped the likes of Phillip McCallen achieve TT success. His son Peter has since proved there is something special in the Hickman racing gene.

My father was a Military Police Sergeant in the army during the war serving in Germany and Holland as a dispatch rider. He didn't talk a lot about what happened during that time so I sense the conflict changed him a lot.

My brother also had a bike when he was in the service and still rode when he became a civvy. I've always had an interest in two wheels. My Dad had a sidecar when I was a youngster but I would never ride in it, I wanted to be and was always on the back of the bike.

By the age of 12, I'd got my hands on a wheelbarrow full of bits and pieces. My own son would more or less copy me doing this years later. I'd seen people riding motorbikes, always fancied having a go, I enjoyed riding push bikes but I liked the look of motorbikes better. I searched locally and found a lad who'd scrapped a bike, so I bought it off him with my pocket money and went on to build the thing which took about six months. It was a 1947 Matchless 350, rigid rear-end tele-forks, you could say it was a big motorcycle for a 12 year old but, without anyone else's help, I'd got it running. I'd had to learn all by myself as my father wasn't mechanically minded and he was insistent that if I wanted to do something, I would have to do it myself. You could say I was the same with my own son, in fact, I was even stricter with him in his early days.

It turned out the bike was a heap of rubbish but the main thing was I'd got it going and learned the basic mechanics along the way, essentially, how to make things work.

I'd also taken an interest in racing by this point. I was either listening to coverage on the radio or reading bits and pieces in local papers. Mallory Park wasn't far away from where I lived so as soon as I was old enough to cadge a ride on the back of another motorbike, I went along with a bunch of lads to the circuit and watched the racing. This was the early '60s so we're talking about seeing riders like Phil Read and Bill Ivy but it was another racer around then, Mike Hailwood, who made the biggest impression on me, simply through his consistency. Years later it was Jarno Saarinen, the way he rode a motorcycle was unlike anything I'd seen before. He had style plus he was down to earth. He would slide bikes around corners which no-one else did, pushing the rear end going towards a turn and drift the bike into it, which came from his spell competing in ice racing so he was quite used to it moving underneath him. It didn't seem to bother him at all. In one of the big races at Mallory Park around 1972 or '73, a friend and I made a big banner out of a bedsheet, put It on the end of two poles and we painted Jarno Saarinen and the Finnish flag on it. We'd wave it at him every time he went past. He went on to win the race by something like half a lap and as he was going around Gerrards with the bike drifting, he lifted his hand off, waved at us and carried on past! We just stood there, shocked yet delighted! He was just so good and so different.

By 1964 I was 15 and had left school and started working. When I turned 16 later that year I bought a bike and started going to local race meetings. I'd often be at Darley Moor where I would marshall and would often think, while watching other lads riding, '*I'm sure I can do better than them.*' I enjoyed riding on the road, I was always quick but safe. I'd be on a small bike like a 250 while the lads I was knocking around with had 500s and 650s, Bonnevilles, Triumphs and the like and wherever we went I would always get there first. The first 250 I owned was a BSA but then I got a Honda CB72 Supersport and that thing was superb. I could corner it and brake comfortably, I didn't need to have a powerful engine as it was easy to handle and I was able to outrun everyone even though I was on a smaller machine.

In 1971, I went to the Isle of Man TT for the first time, it was with a group of lads from Burton on Trent, around seven of us. We travelled across on our bikes to watch the races but the trip on the ferry from Liverpool was rough with me at the front of the bloody boat trying, unsuccessfully, not to be sick. We went for race week, stayed in a B&B, most of my mates were on bigger bikes. I had a 305 Honda rather than a 250 while the lads were on Kawasaki 500 triples and 650s etc. When you got off the boat, rode along the seafront in Douglas all you saw were thousands of bikes parked up and lining either side of the road. All that chrome shining made such an impression on me, you couldn't help but fall in love with the place despite the severity of the crossing. I absolutely loved riding around the Mountain course as a punter. It was an eye-opener and if you enjoyed riding bikes then it was just a great place to be.The first laps I did around the Mountain course were fantastic and the last ones even better, if you get my drift! Every day we were out on the circuit somewhere, just riding around, grabbing a hot dog or a pie, whatever was available. At night I didn't do a lot to be honest, the boys would have a drink or two at the bar in the B&B but I preferred to spend my beer money on putting fuel in the tank and doing some more laps so it would be an early night for me so I could get up early the next day and get back out there. The weather that year wasn't particularly good, it was dry some days and wet on others plus of course in those days they raced no matter what the conditions.

Back home, following one meeting at Darley Moor, where I'd been marshalling, myself and a guy called Richard Gamble were riding back to Burton Trent which meant negotiating some very twisty lanes along the route. He was on his Triumph 750 Triple while I was on a cheap old Suzuki Super Six and I had no trouble in outrunning him. I was way, way ahead so I stopped and pulled over. When he arrived I said

"*Richard, we've got to do something about this. we're getting too fast on the roads, it's becoming too dangerous. Let's go to the Dave Dixon Racing School and try out on a track.*" He agreed but I don't think he thought I was too serious yet two weeks later, I'd actually organised it and things went from there. We did a couple of track days, Silverstone with Dave Dixon and then Oulton Park, which had ex-125cc World Champion Stuart Graham, the son of Les, as one of the instructors, He was wonderful, it was a pleasure watching him leaning backwards, turning around on a bike and then pointing me to go left or right or go here, go there.

In the past a couple of the lads I was riding with on the roads, had offered me a converted scrambler to go racing. They'd seen something that I wasn't really aware of but I turned it down because at 18 I wasn't very brave about talking to my father and mother about racing motorbikes. So, although I was offered bikes by somebody else and support to go with it I daren't mention it to my parents. By 1972 I'd moved out and was married, however, I made the decision to buy a motorbike instead of a washing machine so that was that, game over with my first wife. I did have my hands on a T20 Super six Suzuki though. This is how my racing career started and the following year I had my licence and converted it to an open class 250.

I'd also become qualified to work on all sorts of machines. I used to build TVRs for a company called GT cars in Derby, where I was the sole

TVR engineer in the Midlands. I learned my trade on cars so I'd always had a keen eye on them as well as bikes. With the marriage over, I was single, living in my own house, earning around 30 pounds a week, probably less than that but I wanted to try racing so that's what I did and I was soon competing at Cadwell Park and places like that. Everything was second-hand, repaired or modified by myself. I put extra tubes in the chassis to stiffen it, altered the forks and made the engine more competitive. Whereas everybody else had to push their TD2s and TD3s my bike would start instantly. Two-strokes then could be very temperamental, not everybody knew how to start the bikes properly. I could sit across my 250, paddle it off and it would fire straightaway therefore I'd shoot off down the road ahead of the rest of the field. If it was a five-lap race I'd lead for probably the first three laps, then eventually the faster bikes would catch and pass me. Despite this, I'd always end up in the top five, even though I was on a less-powerful modified Suzuki T20.

Financially, there was no money. I was working from 7 in the morning 'til 5.30 In the evening. I was employed by Marston's brewery so I stuck with the 250 for a year with every penny I earned keeping the house ticking over and the rest of it spent on doing the bike which was kept in the front room where I would prepare it. I had an old A55 fleet van I'd bought from the brewery and to transport the bike, I would take the screen off to get it in the back of the van, drive to the circuit for a club meeting or whatever it was, then sleep in the back with it. When the racing was over, I'd drive back and be at work the next day. Work by day, prepare the bike by night ready for the following weekend, It was rare you'd have a two-day meeting they tended to be single. Tyre-wise I'd have two or three throughout the season. When they began to wear down I would get a marker pen and mark tread on the rubber to get through scrutineering. That's how hard things were. It was worth it as success came and I won the ACU Star 250 championship.

I raced at Darley Moor, Mallory Park, Cadwell, Oulton, Brands Hatch. I kept the T20 for just one season, sold it and then bought a Yamaha TD2B which was Kork Ballington's bike. He was in Oxfordshire at the time and had finished in the top six of the World Championship on this TD2B against the TZs. I couldn't afford a TZ so I spoke to Kork, made the deal and then I went on to win the ACU Clubmans championship in 1975 on it. This was against people like Jon Newbold and Austin Hockley, guys who were all on TZs. I was fighting with my drum brakes against their disc brakes and my air-cooled against their water-cooled. I'd become a good scratch rider too. You had to be good on brakes, steering and suspension to get anywhere on a bike that wasn't particularly quick.

I did my first World championship GP race when I competed at Silverstone in the British Grand Prix, I'd bought one of Charlie Williams 250s and lined up against forty-two other riders. In a short space of time I'd gone from Clubmans to Nationals to Grand Prix within four years.

From Club level to National is a big jump so you have to learn quickly to get up with the top boys and from National to International GP is massive. In the first session I was going around Woodcote quite quickly in fifth gear when suddenly I was passed either side by a couple of 250s. I thought to myself, *'Christ, what have I got to do to match these men?'* Up to that point I'd no idea of what I was doing until I saw what the world boys were capable of doing. The gap was huge. It took me until the third session to qualify and match the speeds they were doing but I did. I finished 18th in the race.

Come 1976 I was sponsored by Appleby Glade, Dave Horton was the man responsible. I was the first man he'd sponsored. He said

"you know how to ride a motorbike so why don't you do the Isle of Man?"

I wasn't so sure I could tackle it because it was bigger, faster and different to short circuit work. I was on a TZ250 Yamaha at the time. He then bought a TZ750, one of the first in the country, for me to ride which was the best bike of its type around then.

With a bit of encouragement I agreed to ride the 250 in the Manx Grand Prix which you had to do back then to learn the ropes before you competed in the TT.

I turned up at the beginning of practice week with nothing in terms of preparation, no driving around for a few days getting to know the place. At first, it was a bit daunting setting off in the early mornings as it tended to be foggy, wet and horrible. There was no training as such you turned up and away you went. The bike was kept in a garage in Onchan while I was nearby in a Douglas B&B. I'd collect the bike, chuck it into the van and head off to the paddock.

The first time down Bray Hill, as you'd expect, is an eye-opener. Through the traffic lights without having to stop, keeping it open down the road, it's a big shock when you go over the top and down the hill but that didn't stop me from grinning ear to ear. I can't really say anything negative about the TT course as I enjoyed every minute of it, sitting in the middle of the road just as if I was riding around lanes in Burton or Derbyshire or Staffordshire. They were cracking roads for learning to ride bikes and now here I was, having done my apprenticeship on the roads so to speak and going through lovely swooping corners around the Isle of Man. I felt that I'd naturally taken to it to be quite honest. I did every practice I could do on my 250, just focused on the one bike and doing my own thing. I was keeping myself to myself, which is what I taught Peter as well, and not listen to too many people. Just keep it to yourself, go your own way. Do your own thing.

In terms of learning the circuit I just sat in the middle of the road and whatever came naturally I didn't worry about. What didn't come naturally I tended to go back and focus on them. I borrowed a MZ from someone and had a look around when the roads were open at the bits I wasn't sure of where I didn't feel comfortable. There were a couple of sections that didn't quite click with me. Laurel Bank was one and then the run from Ginger Hall out through the bumpy bits, past the Conkers in the north of the Island where there were adverse cambers, sometimes that was uncomfortable. The Mountain section wasn't too bad especially if the weather was nice and you could see what you were doing. There are several corners up there that look the same and you need to know which ones are which so I did focus a bit on the Mountain as well.

Come the race I set off, went as quickly as I thought was necessary for

"We started off with a 400-4 road bike and I ended up finishing eighth on it in a 500cc race at Cadwell Park against the likes of Derek Chatterton and Tony Rutter."

DAVID HICKMAN

me and what I was comfortable with. So I sat in the middle and picked the road off as it came and I ended up tenth which I was happy with but even more delighted that I'd finished. That was my goal when I set off, to get to the end. I wasn't a risk taker, that was never part of my game. Conditions in that first year in 1976 were okay, the following year not so.

By that time, I'd left the brewery, as I wanted to race a lot more than I was already doing. I was already 250cc champion and riding in Grand Prix but Marstons still weren't interested, they wouldn't help out. So there was nothing to it, I jacked it in which no-one ever did with a position like that. No-one did that back then, it was a job for life. I was working on transport, in the garage, repairing everything and anything with wheels from forklifts right the way through to Artics, putting them through their MOT. They responded by saying '*you don't pack in a job with the brewery,*' but I told them I wasn't happy and I wanted to pursue a career in sport. I went to work for Brian Crighton running his Honda workshop and because of that I rode his bike at the Manx when I returned twelve months later. Brian developed the engine, I helped out with the chassis setting. We started off with a 400-4 road bike and I ended up finishing eighth on it in a 500cc race at Cadwell Park against the likes of Derek Chatterton and Tony Rutter. We realised there was potential with the machine so we bored it to 500 and took it to the Manx. It was a busy fortnight riding two bikes.

Brian and myself were the two spanner men. He did most of the work on the 500 while I prepared the Maxton Yamaha 250. We decided to change the piston rings on the bigger bike halfway through practice week but the oil we were using wouldn't allow the engine to run in so we had to swap it back to the old piston rings. It was also the first time we tried an infrared Piranha ignition system yet every time we went out the bike broke down, so we ended up putting points and condensers back on and went back to a standard ignition system, bearing in mind I was revving the thing to 13 and a half thousand, which was going off the clock. I was full throttle going down Bray Hill on both the 250 and the 500. Everyone was always eager to drop down there flat out but rarely did. Shell used to rent a house halfway down Bray Hill and the rep who worked for Michelin tyres watched from there and told me I was the only guy keeping the throttle on the bike '*flat chat*' all the way through. I just thought '*you need to go quick and you don't do that if you shut it off.*'

It was a very different circuit than the one today, certainly a lot bumpier. Quarry Bends is a high speed swoop now but in my day it was a set of badly cambered s-bends. It was very bumpy as you went in and out of the trees. The light would be flickering through the leaves on the overhanging branches. You couldn't take it at any great speed because you'd come through the trees and the darkness plus the negative cambers so if you got the line wrong it would run you wide into the kerbs. The bumps seemed to get worse the further north you went.

During practice we got the Crighton Honda to third quickest so we were in a good place at that point. Nobody could believe it was a converted 400-4. Brian acquired the Martin Sharpe Spartan chassis where we grafted the Honda engine into it. I did a few modifications and rode my heart out to make it work. Brian produced a good engine with a Futura cam and some factory carburetors and four separate handmade exhaust pipes. The noise was incredible. Just like listening to the factory Honda or the MV roaring round in your ear from years past. It was inspiring. Unfortunately, my race came to a premature end when the bike threw a rod out of the front as I approached Braddan bridge on lap three. That was a pain in the backside. For that to happen was unfortunate, it had so much potential. We put the highest gearing on it that we had, which was from the road bike, then we scrounged around for sprockets to try and make it taller still, as I was peaking out on the rpm. Crighton built a really super Honda engine. It wasn't overly quick but because it drove everywhere in any gear, it was easy to ride.

The Maxton Yamaha had also gone quick in practice, I was in the top two all the way through the week when Ron Williams of Maxton came to see me just before the last practice session. He had this new monoshock shock absorber he'd developed and asked if I'd like to try it. So we stuck it in, it felt okay so decided to leave it in for the race. I went on to win so

Ron and I have been friends ever since. I kept it for the rest of the season.

The day the race was due to go there were high winds and rain with twigs and branches all over the road. They'd just surfaced the area going into School corner so there was freshly-laid gravel; nobody had been on the bloody thing. The conditions were so poor they delayed it. We had to take our bikes to Mylchreests Garage to put into storage. Nobody's allowed to touch them. The race might have actually been delayed for two days. When we went to collect the bike for the rescheduled race day I realised I had to change the fuel in the bike but at first, they wouldn't let me, I wasn't allowed to touch the bike. So, I told the official *"look, the fuel's now lost its octane rating, it's had oil in it for up to two days or more and therefore the octane rating's dropped and it'll detonate itself to death if I don't change it. Are you willing to pay for my funeral? Are you willing to pay for the bits in the bike?"*

Anyway, I changed the fuel at the risk of getting penalised for it and started the race. Halfway around I had a pit signal at somewhere like Ramsey that said 'P1' which was encouraging to say the least. It was a four-lapper so I pulled in on the third to fuel up. Unfortunately, the lads who were fuelling for me, didn't measure how much they were putting in. Going into the pits I was about a minute and a half ahead of second place. With fuel onboard I rejoined the race but as it went on, the weather changed and the temperature got warmer. The last time going up the mountain, the bike shut down onto one cylinder and began running richer on the climb. I'd erred on the side of caution and gone with a grade harder plug plus a size bigger jet than I'd normally use just to make sure it finished the distance therefore the bike was a bit sluggish. Now with just one cylinder over the mountain I was turning the fuel taps off, getting it back on to two-cylinders then switching them back on. When they died I would switch the fuel back on again and go once more. You can hear it on the mountain, the change in tone. The engine note changed as I rode up from Ramsey hairpin. I got firing properly around the 33rd milestone and from there I went as hard as I could to try to get the time back so when I finished the race, I was only three seconds ahead of second place, which was Richard Swallow. The newspaper headline read '*Hickman's win was hard to Swallow.*' I'd gone from over a minute and a half lead down to three seconds by the time we finished.

The other thing of note is that I started at number 73 and yet I finished second on the road. If it hadn't been messed about, the bike would have finished first because I could see somebody in front of me as I crossed the line. I was picking riders off here, there and everywhere. There's some super photos about where I'm going around the outside of people at Ginger Hall. I remember thinking '*I wish they would get out of the way*' as I couldn't go where I wanted to and by that I mean remaining safe and quick. It was quite a ride which I thoroughly enjoyed.

Crossing the finish line I was bubbling up all over. It was just incredible, absolutely incredible. Everybody was cheering, yelling and shouting especially as I'd come from 73rd to 2nd on the road, people were wanting me to sign this and that. I was taken into the office to be told '*we've a lot of requests for your autograph*'. We used to have stick-on number plates then and I was signing them. It was a very big pack of about 50 but the whole experience was phenomenal. When I was on the podium and holding the trophy aloft, the man who presented it to me was none other than John H. 'Crasher' White who'd ridden for Norton in the 1930s. He turned to me and said

"*I don't know how you do what you do?*"

So I replied

"*Hang on a second, forty years ago you did 90-odd miles an hour with no more than 30 brake horsepower on roads much worse than this often in far from ideal conditions? I don't know how you managed that!*'"

In the evening we had the reception at the Villa Marina. I was carried into the hall on the chair at shoulder height. They were bouncing me up and down on this thing onto the stage. It was absolutely wonderful, Brian Crighton was with me, along with a couple of other blokes who had also come to the Island, one of which was Brian Slack who used to build engines for myself and Charlie Williams.

Of course, once you'd won the Manx Grand Prix you can't take part in it again so it was onto the TT the next year and what a time to be in it. 1978. The return of Mike Hailwood!

The Island was buzzing. He'd come back out of retirement so the atmosphere was incredible, the sun just seemed to shine all the time that year. I met Mike in the paddock. I was preparing my bike, waiting to go out into the assembly area after scrutineering and Mike was standing next me with his Martini Yamaha and we were just chatting away. I'm thinking *'I can't believe I used to watch this guy during the '60s, thinking he was some sort of God and now he is next to me chattering away just like one of the boys.'* He was a great fella who I got to meet a few times over the fortnight.

I went there with Appleby Glade on my 250 and I also had a 350 if I wanted it but the plan was to stick to the smaller bike. Meanwhile, the Jawa factory team were making a comeback in not just Grand Prix but road racing as well and during practice week they offered me the ride on their 250 which I accepted. So I had to break the news to Dave Horton from Appleby Glade that I'd no longer be riding his bike, which wasn't pleasant. For the previous 18 months I'd been helping out Jawa on the short circuits, testing with them at Cadwell, Mallory and also Oulton Park with Eddie Roberts and Tom Herron. Dave wasn't best pleased I wouldn't be riding his bike but I explained I'd been helping out Jawa and wanted to continue to do so especially as I felt the bikes had potential. So, he reluctantly let me go. Eddie Roberts was the other rider in the Jawa team for the TT. He was riding Grand Prix for them along with Peter Balaz who didn't want to do the TT so they asked me to fill in.

Knocking back Dave Horton is one of the things I regret but it's difficult when you get offered an opportunity to be involved with a company like Jawa. No matter how small it was, it's still a factory team with a massive history. I'd watched Bill Ivy years before on the 350 and that had stuck in my mind. The 250 had the best designed engine I've ever seen, absolutely brilliant. A cracking little engine but they hadn't got Nikasil plated barrels, they had iron liner barrels in aluminium casings which were pretty terrible. It was a disc-valve engine which I'd previously worked on but unfortunately, during the race, it broke down several times. The clutch broke so there were bits hitting my foot, the water pump seal went so I've got water and oil also flying about so I had to stop several times to wipe things off my boots and check the bike to make sure it was safe enough to keep going but I finished the distance and got a bronze replica for my troubles. I'd used a long tank on it as I thought the short one wouldn't be the best option. Eddie disagreed with me but he may have changed his mind when I passed him as he was pushing up from Hillberry to Signpost. I couldn't resist giving him a little wave as I went by! I finished the race in 31st. My aim was to make it to the end so I was happy with that. Later that year I also raced for them at the Grand Prix races at Silverstone and then Czechoslovakia where I ended up 14th, which was the best result they'd had since Billy Ivy was riding for them.

On the short circuits that year I was running the single-cylinder Honda in the Shellsport 125cc British Championship and was top three in that. I was also campaigning in the Vladivar 250cc British Championship alongside the likes of Clive Padgett, again I was top three in that series. By then, I was riding for Coventry-based Oxford Road Service Station and my team-mates were Chas Mortimer and Takazumi Katayama who went back to Japan, leaving his factory YZR750. Chas wouldn't ride it so I had a go. I was always in the top five.

In 1979 everything changed.

Dorothy Whitehouse had a rider called Ian Richards who decided he wasn't going to ride her bikes anymore as they were too old and not competitive. So, they were offered to me and I agreed to ride her 250cc and 350cc machines and she said if I went well then she'd buy me a Suzuki 500 RG.

The bikes were three-years-old, they'd been developed by Ian during that time and on my first outing on them I won. That was at Cadwell followed by Mallory and Dorothy was over the moon. She was a proper old queen in the paddock, always dressed in black with black-dyed hair. She was something of an old lady but a proper character and would often smother me in red lipstick.

I hadn't gone to the Isle of Man that year because they wouldn't pay me enough to bring the bike. I'd applied to go, spoken with the organisers and they said, if you bring a 750 as well as the 250 we'll help by giving you 300 pounds. This clearly wasn't enough as it wouldn't cover the cost of the tyres for the 250 let alone the 750. So I told them I can't do it, I won't do it plus the 750's were quite an animal. I thought it was too much of a handful, one slight mistake or one inch the wrong way and you're gone with it. So I decided not to go and instead concentrated on the post-TT at Mallory Park and followed that by racing in Europe with Chas Mortimer and Takazumi at some of the internationals in Holland and Belgium.

At Mallory I was fastest in practice so I was in pole position. We did a warm up lap and as we finished that and pulled up onto the grid the TV camera crew came along and started doing interviews with the riders while the bikes were still running on the bloody grid. It wasn't long before my bike started boiling over so I ended up being second or third from last to get away, which was disappointing. I was just blown away from the start because I couldn't get the bike cleared out. By the end of the first lap I was up to around 23rd but five or six laps later I had pushed through to fourth place. I broke the lap record several times and had just passed Steve Henshaw and Peter Labuschagne going into Gerard's. I passed one around the outside, the other on the inside and then pulled it in tight to try and avoid the ripples on the exit of Gerard's but I just caught the edge of them and away the bike went. I hung onto it until I got to the edge, flicked it out of the way and then slid down the track. Unfortunately, the two lads I just passed were right behind me and there was nothing they could do with both going over the top of me.

I broke everything from my neck to my knees. I remember every minute of it. It all seemed to happen in slow motion too. On the exit out of Gerard's onto the back straight I was travelling along on my backside without the bike so I put my hands down to slow myself down and Steve Henshaw said to me afterwards,

"I was praying you wouldn't put your hands down because I was so close to you and as soon as you did I clipped you and went through you."

Pete Labuschagne was still behind as I went sideways across the track, he couldn't help but hit me and rolled over the top of my body, still on his bike and disappeared into the crowd. I think he fractured his ankle but I ended up with my left leg around the back of my head. All of my ribs had burst. I had a broken pelvis, spine, neck and where Steve hit me in the shoulder I've still got a boot mark.

I was in Leicester Royal hospital for 18 months and it was absolute hell. It's amazing how much you get used to hospital food and thinking how good it is, until you get back home again and you realise how bad it was.

It was a difficult time. The newspaper reported that I had a broken leg. They didn't say that it was attached to five pieces of pelvis, five vertebrae in the spine and neck, both shoulders, all but two of the ribs, lungs, kidneys, my left leg from the knee to the ball joint was broken into 30 small pieces. I was in from June until December when they sent me out in a massive hip spica which is a body plaster from the chest down to your feet, reinforced with steel so you couldn't break it. They sent me out of hospital for three months to try and get my head straight, stop me from going stir crazy. I ended up having to go back to the hospital where they started cracking the joints in an effort to make me mobile but when they stood me up all of my toenails blew off. That was because they'd bled so much from the pressure inside my feet. When I tried to walk, my leg just snapped around so I was back into the ward again. They discussed taking the leg off but I wouldn't let them. Eventually they brought in a specialist called Mr. Chan, who's now a professor. He rebuilt the leg by putting in 12 titanium screws, a titanium plate, bone grafted the 30 pieces together and a large titanium bolt in there to secure everything. The leg is three-inches shorter than the right one but I've still got it and I'm still using it. My pelvis and back give me a bit of pain but I'm getting on as well so it's only to be expected.

I recovered slowly but as soon as I could walk on crutches I set about getting back to work. I teamed up with John Davis, who I'd been involved with before and he gave me a job in a motorcycle shop as well as his car place. Then along came Peter Hubbard and a local lad, Steve Thompson, who had a RDV disc-valve Yamaha 250.

He was building the engine but they were breaking every time so I ended up building and preparing them with him. I then worked for Capitol Racing from 1982 to '84 when they sponsored Steve so I carried on spannering for him as he competed in the European championship along with Pete. I also did the driving and more or less ran the team. I was finding it tough not being able to race myself but my enjoyment was now through pointing them in the right direction. I'd learned a lot about carburation, chassis and engine setups, all those sorts of things over the years and as a mechanic, I'd always been interested in that side of motorcycles. I could build a good motorcycle and a quick one. In fact, Peter was MCN Starmaker 250cc champion in 1984, on the Capital Racing Rotax. This was wonderful for me as it meant I stayed in the racing game.

Next was a stint with Silverstone Armstrong; Chas Mortimer was team manager. This was the time of the carbon 250s that Niall McKenzie and Donnie McLeod rode. I was then poached by Dr. Joseph Ehrlich for EMC. He was a specialist engine-tuner who'd emigrated to the U.K. from Austria around the 1930s and '40's and he made unique two-strokes. I ended up building a lot of bikes for the Irish lads who loved the EMC machines as they were fast. I was doing Grand Prix racing with the likes of Andy Watts, Gary Knowle, and Donnie McLeod who'd also switched to EMC. I prepared a 125 for Alan Scott and this was the first that became the Aprilia 125. I spent a couple of weeks in Gunskirchen in Austria with Rotax building the first of the 125's with twin-discs and mono-chassis.

My Grand Prix and European championship adventures finished at the end of 1987 as I needed to be at home more. Brian Crighton was playing with rotary engines and that winter he invited me to have a look at what he was up to. Cut a long story short I joined up and we entered the air-cooled Nortons in the Isle of Man TT in 1988. They were modified road bike engines which Norton had scrapped and we reclaimed. We fastened them together and sent them off around short circuits and then the TT in the hands of Simon Buckmaster and Trevor Nation. We needed to prove the bike, with a rotary engine, could go the distance and they did. We actually got them to finish, which was the main objective as we knew we couldn't win anything, the bike was nowhere near developed properly. Another thing that was developing at the time was my son, Peter, he came to the TT in 1988 as a one-year-old. We worked in a garage behind the Castle Mona hotel in Douglas where we stayed that year and had just been refurbished. The bikes were ridden up to the paddock from there every morning and back every evening. Try and do that now!

The following year we had JPS backing and won the British Championship but it all came to an end for me in 1990 when the new team manager came in and brought his own guys in. He got rid of Brian straight away and I went too about three months later. That was disappointing because we knew the potential of the bike, we'd already won the MCN and British Supercup championships on it with Steve Spray and Trevor Nation riding. However, the new team wanted to do things their way, which, in my mind, wasn't as good as what we were doing.

Therefore I went back to Grand Prix with Ian McConnachie. This was with Clay Cross Kawasaki and I was now preparing British championship bikes, which were 250cc Production, 250cc GP and 125cc and abroad we were racing in the GP 125cc class. That was a couple of years and then I was reunited with Brian Crighton at the end of '91 and joined his Roton project, which was the rotary engine in the Spondon chassis, which I helped develop and design.

I spent months at Spondon where we designed the aluminium-beam chassis. We began as Roton but became Duckhams Norton in '93 with Jim Moodie and won the British championship with Ian Simpson in 1994 while our other rider, Phil Borley, finished third. The rules changed in '95 so we could no longer run the rotary engine therefore we sold the bikes. Norton was almost closed by then so we were running the Duckhams team virtually on our own. Colin Seeley had been the team manager from '93 and he was approached by Honda to take over their British championship team as Neil Tuxworth, who was in charge, went off to run Honda's World Superbike team. Myself and Brian Crighton went with

Colin and we joined Honda Britain in 1995. This meant working with Phillip McCallen who was wild and I mean that in the nicest way possible. He's the only guy I know to destroy five wheels in one week at the TT. He was hitting kebs, jumping and bouncing off them, throwing the bike around. It seemed every time Phillip brought the bike in, it was bent or there was a wheel gone in fact we had to order in more wheels from Dymag. It was unbelievable but boy, he could ride. We did the NorthWest 200 as well with not only Phillip but Joey Dunlop, Nick Jefferies and Steve Ward. That meant four 750s to prepare which kept us busy. The RC45 was a serious pain in terms of racing. The balance of the bike and the setup of the engine was, as far as I was concerned, all wrong. We wrote a letter to Honda asking them to change into different specs and twin-fork swing-arms instead of the mono, single-sided version. It just didn't suit what we were doing with the bike, the dimensions were all wrong. They replied saying *'Honda built this, it will win'* to which I responded *'not in this form.'* Lo and behold, not long after the bike had a standard type swinging-arm, modifications to the motor and it won.

We stayed with Honda Britain for one season and then Colin, Brian and myself moved onto Ducati as they were winning most things but the bikes weren't staying together very well as the engines weren't particularly strong. Unfortunately for me, I retired part way through the campaign because I couldn't take it anymore, I was physically breaking down a lot of the time. We had five engines, two bikes and we couldn't keep on top of it. I couldn't go on anymore. My bodywork wasn't good. My spine and legs were giving me a lot of stick. I was collapsing in the workshop while carrying wheels across the room and I couldn't get back up on my own. The lads would find me in a heap on the floor so they'd pick me up and put me in a chair and I'd wait 'til I recovered a bit but I couldn't carry on like that so I retired from work completely.

Years later, Peter took an interest in racing which was entirely his own doing. I wouldn't let him near anything on two wheels. Then, when he was 12 years old, just like me, he bought a wheelbarrow full of bits. I came home one day and my remote-control competition glider was missing and there was a wheelbarrow full of rusty bits and pieces in its place. He'd saved his pocket money and swapped the glider so he could get his hands on this stuff. I left him alone for a few weeks while he was in tears trying to put this thing together yet he wouldn't give up.

The one thing my wife Sue and I didn't want him doing was go racing. From the age of ten we had him playing football, judo, cross-country running, swimming, every single thing we could to stop him riding motorbikes. What does he end up doing? He just wanted to ride a bike and we couldn't stop him.

Just down the road from where we were in Willoughby, Lincolnshire, there was a chap who used to race called John Kirkby. He rode Laverda 125 and 250s and had seen Peter tinkering and mucking about with bikes in our next door neighbour's yard. Now he had a friend called Phil Kirkham whose son Will was racing mini bikes, he owned two or three but they kept breaking down so I ended up spannering these little machines. Unbeknown to me they'd taken Peter to a minimoto meeting, just to go along to watch. When they came back he said to me *'You should see your lad on two wheels'* and I was like *'Oh no!'* All this time we'd been fighting this, it wasn't what I wanted to hear. He said if I looked after the bikes then Peter and his lad could ride them and we'll see where it goes. There was no going back so we called ourselves Man-hat-on racing, Phil's company. The following year he bought a pair of 125s to take part in the Aprilia Superteen Challenge. So Peter did a year on a minimoto and then a season on the 125 with me again on the spanners. Stuart Hicken, who founded Hawk Racing, then spotted him at Mallory Park and was so impressed he bought him a Kawasaki 400 to race on for the following season. There was no stopping him and he eventually went on to ride in the British Superbike championship.

Peter was a BSB regular when, one night, he decided to take Sue and I out for a meal. We were thinking *'there's something cooking here. He's never, ever done this before. What's going on?'* By the end of the evening, I kicked his shins, I said,

"Come on, Pete, what's going on?"

We'd had all three courses and a coffee, before he mentioned anything about the TT. That year, he didn't have a permanent ride in BSB. So he said

"I want to stretch my wings a bit and have a look at some road racing."

I said,

"*What* are you talking about?"

to which he replied,

"I'm going to have a look at the TT."

"When are you going?"

"Tomorrow."

The bugger had it all organised so there was no way of me talking him out of it.

To say I was unhappy was an understatement. I'd told him before that I wouldn't talk to him or spanner his bikes, if he went to the roads or TT because it takes a particular type of mental attitude for that type of racing. I'd done a lot of road riding before I raced. I knew I could cope with that. I didn't know what Peter could cope with. I knew he was quick to learn circuits and he could ride pretty much anything up to a pretty good level but the TT is totally different. Over the years, I'd lost a few friends to road racing so I wasn't keen on him doing it, not even Scarborough let alone the TT.

As parents that's how we felt but our attitudes changed when we saw how he approached things. He went there racing on Paul Shoesmith's Ice Valley bike, we'd met him in the Superstock championship where they'd raced against each other. Paul had ridden it at the TT the year before, Pete's crew chief Darren Jones came along too and worked on the machine with another lad while I did suspension set up, dampening the spring to suit the road. That was the start of Pete's TT adventure. I'm stunned by just how good he is. It's breathtaking. I've been over there. I know what it takes to go quickly. I know how fast it looks when you watch the videos. It's happening so fast and he will sit there next to me and talk me through every bump, every corner, every drain top and it's going so fast, I can't take it in. It's like a nice Sunday run for him. Even when he is on the grid ready to go along Glencrutchery Road, his hat's off, he's smiling, chattering away; it's like he's supposed to be there. When the race is over he is chilled, he doesn't look rushed, he's barely broken into a sweat. Meanwhile, Sue and I are sitting in the Grandstand shaking! The first time we went Sue never spoke to me for the entire fortnight. She was terrified. That first year in 2014 I told Pete I had to go along just to make sure the bike was right before he went out, particularly on the big bikes. It has to be right. Over the later years, I've passed on some of my knowledge and experience onto Darren and he has taken it on from there even further, which is great. Whenever I speak to him and say '*Daz, have you done this or that?*' and he always replies '*Look, already done.*'

Peter getting his first TT win was absolutely stunning. Breathtaking. I couldn't believe it. We were in that much of a panic to get down to the presentation area I'd forgotten where to go. I was dashing left, right and in my rush to get there had even left Sue behind. I got there, jumped over the fence into the assembly area where the top three come in. It was a very emotional experience.

Then, of course, came the 135mph lap in the Senior TT 2018. I had my earphones on, sat in the Grandstand, listening to the commentary, with a stopwatch in my hand. We knew when he came out of the pits after fuelling for the last time that he had a lot of people in front of him on the road. I remember thinking '*This is going to be tough,*' but halfway around he was up on his times. I was watching the timing, clicking my stopwatch and I said to Sue,

"There's a 136 on here if he gets a clear run."

When he crossed the line and it was announced he'd broken the lap record everybody was really shocked. It was stunning. He absolutely blew it out of the water, which is amazing. Absolutely bloody amazing. I still can't believe it. I was just praying he kept it safe and passed the other riders safely, which he did. It's incredible thinking back to it. It's the biggest experience anybody could ever have, something really unique. It's special. I've got a little plaque on the wall at home, which says 135.452. Both Sue and I are very, very proud of him.

Since retirement David and his wife Sue continue to live in Louth, Lincolnshire. They go to every race meeting Peter's involved with often spending a few extra days either side of the racing. When he's not supporting his son, David can often be found casting a rod into water and is Chairman of his local fishing club.

JASON GRIFFITHS

Usk, Wales

TT Years 1992-2006
60 races, 4 x 2nd, 9 x 3rd, 7 x 4th, 8 x 5th, 9 x 6th, 3 x 7th, 1 x 8th, 2 x 9th, 2 x 10, 1 x 15th, 1 x 18th 13 x DNF

MGP 1991, 1999-2003
8 races, 3 x 1st, 1 x 2nd, 1 x 3rd, 4 x DNF

Along with Roger Marshall and Guy Martin, Jason Griffiths is always part of the '*greatest riders never to win a TT*' debate. The Welshman may not have been a multiple British champion or a TV superstar but his record in the Isle of Man is up there with the best. An astonishing 37 top six finishes in 60 TT races is a statistic to be proud of, in fact of all those he finished he failed to make the top 10 just twice. Often praised for his smooth riding style, he was unfortunate not to make it onto the top of a TT podium.

My father Selwyn raced primarily during the 60s and kept riding up until about the mid 1970s. He worked for Ray Cowles who sponsored a lot of big TT names, John Hartle and Brian Reid spring to mind, Ian Lougher, Robert Dunlop as well, they all rode his bikes as did my dad.

Being the son of a racer it would be easy to be accused of being pushed into it but it was entirely my choice. I'd ridden around fields from about the age of 7, which isn't that early in comparison to these days but it was just fun up until about 13 when I did schoolboy motocross for a couple of years. I then drifted away from it around 1987 and the next time I competed was when I began road racing having just left my teenage years behind.

I often went to the TT as a youngster as it was our annual family holiday. This was the mid-70s so I would have been around 5 years old. Dad stopped racing at Cadwell Park and all those sorts of short circuits when his kids came along. By then, it was pretty much just the TT he concentrated on.

My earliest TT memory isn't anything romantic like being sat on the winner's bike as a child or something similar but in fact being hit by a swing just above my eye and having a horrendous gash which needed stitches. This was more than likely in Nobles Park playground close to the paddock. Going to the Isle of Man was always an adventure, sitting in the back of a small van full of motorcycles. I would often be lying down between them trying to sleep. I can still smell the bikes, the oil or whatever it was that filled the air as we made the journey to the Island and eventually our digs at a guest house in Woodburn Square, Douglas. Dad stopped racing for around a dozen years or so but returned in the late '80s doing events like the Classic Manx Grand Prix. That whole Forgotten Era scene started up around then and he enjoyed being part of it.

I went with him to the Isle of Man for the Pre-TT Classic in 1989. That was on the Billown course in the south of the Island and took place on the weekend before TT practice week. We were only there for a few days so took the opportunity to watch early morning practice on the Monday at the Creg ny Baa then it was down to the pits on Glencrutchery Road for the evening session. It's something I'll never forget as I got to sit on Steve Hislop's RC30, albeit very briefly, which became the bike that he did the first 120 mile an hour lap on a day or two later. Hizzy's brother Gary had ridden for Ray Cowles so that was our connection. I also spent a minute or two chatting with Steve and I can't stress enough how much of an impression he made on me which really sowed my interest in motorcycle road racing.

In 1990 Ray Cowles bought a new 250 Yamaha for Ian Lougher to ride, a TZ250A reverse cylinder. It was first raced at the Northwest 200 that year where he finished second and soon after Ian unofficially broke the TT lap record by eighteen seconds during practice. He then went on to have that really great race with Steve Hislop where he tore twenty seconds off the lap record as he and Hizzy battled away. It was especially exciting for me as I did the fuel at the pitstop. Having that responsibility you want to be as quick as you can but you can't rush it, you have to make sure there is enough fuel to do the last two laps. It's such a basic operation, making sure you don't spill any then putting the cap back on tightly but with the added pressure of knowing the slightest mistake can be costly. Ian went on to win by just one point eight seconds from Steve with the pair of them head and shoulders ahead of a quality field including the likes of Carl Fogarty, Eddie Laycock, Phillip McCallen and Johnny Rea. Strange to think too that Hizzy was such a 250 specialist, in fact winning the British championship, and yet never winning on one at the TT. That was the closest he came. It would also be another nine years before any 250 went faster again at the isle of Man.

I then did my first ever race in July 1990. It was at Darley Moor and it was on that TT winning bike. I was lapped by Jimmy Brown in one of those early races, he was a good 250 rider at National level and I thought to myself '*how can anyone ride that fast?*' I was steady on the bike, I certainly wasn't wild but I came away scratching my head as to how I was struggling on a proven TT winner. Darley's quite a peculiar place with those long straights and tight chicanes. The next meeting quickly followed at Castle Combe, organised by the North Gloucester club. That was a really hot day with a lot of riders. Two strokes were still popular at the time with 250 and 350s making for some very big grids. The track there is fast and flowing but quite bumpy. It was a while until my next race meeting which was towards the end of the year. I did a few around then and took a tumble at Park corner at Cadwell, thankfully only a minor one which didn't put me off. Through the winter things began to click and I started to get some decent results. This was all at club level and going into the next season it all felt much easier so I started to focus my attention on racing a bit more than I had been doing. We were quite fortunate in that Phil Davis, the circuit manager of Pembrey was very helpful in allowing us track time to run bikes in if we had things to do like rebuilds. There's truth in the old story, there's no substitute for circuit time. So I did a lot of laps around Pembrey which helped an awful lot.

I got rid of my novice jacket and around late February, early March I was on the grid at a very cold Snetterton. Ray Cowles was now running Robert Dunlop on one of the first of the V-twin Yamaha TZ250 B for 1991. We also went to Northern Ireland for the Cookstown and Tandragee meetings where Robert rode the bikes before taking the 250 to victory at the North West 200. He was also riding the Norton in the big bike classes but unfortunately broke his collarbone at Donington Park just before the TT.

Next was the Isle of Man. We were now staying at Roger Sutcliffe's house in Douglas. He was a Manx Grand Prix winner as was his son Ralph; their victories both on Ray Cowles machinery. Robert did limited practice during the week because he was struggling to take part so the night before the race he came up with the idea of turning the handlebars upside down. We swapped them from side to side so they became almost like a cowhorn bar. It was a real suck it and see job, we just made sure everything worked, all the cable runs were good and nothing was fouling.

Come race day Robert was at number four and Philip McCallen at two. Robert, in his usual style, would always think about how he was going to approach the race and went on to have a great ride. He closed in on Phillip going up the Mountain mile so he knew he had a gap over him which he kept to the chequered flag plus it was a second consecutive Junior TT win for Ray Cowles. It was great for me too as I did the refuelling once more while Robert's Norton team-mate Ron Haslam was on visor wiping duty. We ended the week with my first ever road race when I competed at the Post-TT at Billown. Not ideal conditions, it was wet but I rode the 250 to a top six finish.

The following month I did my first ever Irish road race when we went to Skerries followed by Faugheen. Robert was riding his TT winning bike while I was on Lougher's winner from the year before.

I also had an entry for that year's Manx Grand Prix. Bob Heath had agreed I could ride his RC30 which was sort of an ex-Honda Britain machine and it was lovely. Carl Fogarty had used the engine at Daytona and the Koni shock absorber in the back was the one Hizzy had when he did his 120 mile an hour lap a couple of years earlier. So the bike had a lot of pedigree, it was a beautiful piece of kit. This was such a massive step for me because I never rode it on the track before the Manx. Times were a bit different back then. We did a lot of the running in at a certain locality of South Wales where I lived. It may have been on public roads, I couldn't possibly say! I rode it most evenings because the engine needed bedding. I put in around a couple of hundred miles but never rode it in anger.

So I went to the Manx with the 250 Yamaha and felt ready in terms of the way I'd prepared.

I'd been riding all year, spent a lot of time with Robert Dunlop which helped and physically, I put quite a lot into it as well. I built the year around it really. The 250 was the bike Robert had won on that year and I entered the 750 newcomers class with the RC 30.

I arrived a few days before spending most of my free time going around the course in a van. I would stop and walk certain sections, places I thought could be tricky, like Rhen Cullen. I would go both ways; walk through and back again. I'd look at where you thought you'd be peeling off and where the kerbs were, that sort of thing. it stuck in my mind fairly well. I always thought I was reasonable at learning and retaining information for road racing no matter where it was.

I was steady through practice, didn't push too hard at all, just took my time. I actually slipped off the 250 in Thursday afternoon practice at Ramsey hairpin. It was very innocuous, slipping off the side of it, picking it back up and going again. It was a great year to make my Mountain debut as we had incredible weather although there was one occasion where they stopped us in Parliament Square and led us back over the mountain because it was misty. Apart from that it was stinking hot for two weeks.

My Dad was also there riding a classic bike. We would have been in the same sessions as the Newcomers went out with the old machinery plus I was lucky again to have the help of Steve Hislop. He was living on the island by that time so would watch practice in the evenings and later would put me right on a few things he'd noticed. He was always a friendly character, very approachable. After I'd sat on his bike in 1989 I saw him one evening at that year's Weston Super Mare beach race which he was taking part in so went across, said '*hello do you remember me*?' which he did and he was spot on, very friendly. He was the man at the TT then of course. I also met him when I went to Hockenheim with Ian Lougher who was doing the European Championship while Steve was doing 250 Euros. We were all Brits together in the paddock. Robert was there on a 125 in his old PJ O'Kane bus which he used to use. There were all sorts of characters around the paddock guys like Woolsey Coulter and Alan Patterson. So by the time of the Manx I knew Hizzy quite well.

Robert came over to the Island and, returning the favour somewhat, helped out in my pitstop for the Newcomers race. We were starting in pairs back then and I went at number six. I took the lead which was pleasing especially considering the opposition, strong riders such as Tim Leach plus Graham Ward who finished on the podium and now works with Michael Rutter. Also in the Newcomers race that day and someone who became a very good friend, was Nick Morgan of top British racing team MSS performance. Everything went perfectly as I took the win, recording a new lap record for the class as well.

Next it was the Junior Manx Grand Prix and I was number 95. This was on the Wednesday and I was in sixth place on the last lap when the chain jumped off the sprockets as I went through Parliament Square. So that was the end of that one. Onto Friday morning, this time I had a really good number which I have Clerk of the Course Jack Wood to thank for. Having been number 95 in the Junior I was then placed at two in the Lightweight. That helped as I had a good ride and went on to finish second behind Dave Milling. who was something of a MGP regular with a lot more circuit experience than me so was always going to be difficult to beat. So I had a really good week coming away with the 750 Newcomers win and second on the 250. I could have done the Manx again the following year but wanted to step up to do the TT.

Everyone knows about the dangers of the TT. I was always a steady type of a rider and I have a vague recollection of coming on to Glencrutchery Road to start my first ever flying lap and wondering just how bad is this gonna be. To be fair it was all sort of manageable on the 250 whereas when you're really pushing it on the bigger bikes it changes things but by then you're more experienced. I'd been lucky to have had a couple of Irish races under my belt as well as spending a lot of time with Robert and I would say to this day, he was somebody who really thought a lot about racing so some of the tips and advice he gave always put you in good stead. He had a great understanding of the bike and how to ride it, so it was a real benefit to learn from him.

My schoolboy motocross background certainly helped in terms of road racing. I think it gave me a good starting point, racing over bumps, putting your weight on the foot rests, not necessarily holding the handlebars too tight. When I stayed with Roger Sutcliffe, he was one of the first people that took me around which he did with a lot of newcomers. He had a particular way of reinforcing things, he'd say *'this is what happened to so and so here'* so he made sure that I thought about my approach to that first Manx Grand Prix. One of Robert's sayings was *'do the fast parts faster and the slow parts slower'*. It's a bit of an oversimplification but puts it into perspective; you need to take care in some places and make up time in others

Another step was competing in the British 250 championships. Then it was the Supercup plus the ACU championship which meant a lot of races. A very strong group of riders too on those 250cc grids. You had Paul 'Marra' Brown, Nigel Bosworth, Ian Newton, Jeremy McWilliams, Steve Sawford and Mark Barker. Kevin Mitchell, in between riding GPs plus Alan Carter at times on the Honda UK bike. Ian McConnaughey was back having competed at Grand Prix. The level in the UK was incredibly high, the racing was great but incredibly tough.

At the time if I wasn't working in Ray Cowles bike shop I was away racing. I didn't have money for anything else. Work during the week and race at the weekend. Good fun.

Having decided to do the TT I put in my entry for 1992 with the same bikes, the 250 and the RC30. This was also the year of Hizzy on his Norton and Foggy on Rob McElnea's Yamaha.

I went out quite early on the 250 for the first practice on Monday morning and felt quite nervous as it was the TT. Carl Fogarty on what could have been the V&M Yamaha 400 gave me an early alarm call when he flew past as we approached Glen Helen. Brian Reid was another that passed me early on the first lap. I was feeling my way around the circuit again but they were on it straight away. I'd see them for two corners and they'd be gone.

My race week started well, finishing tenth in the Formula One. Next was the Junior and I have just one recollection of that race. I don't recall where I finished but I will never forget Steve Hislop on the Padgett's Yamaha passing me at the top of Barregarrow. It was just mind blowing. I didn't really know what happened, he just seemed to suck the paint off the side of my bike as he went past. Everything about it was sort of perfect, which, I guess, was what he was. I only saw him heading down through the bottom of Barregarrow and maybe a little bit along the approach to the 13th milestone before he was gone. That's clear in my mind because he started at number 19.

Everyone talks about the Hizzy-Foggy Senior and quite rightly so. I was having a mega ride and looking good for a top six finish in the race, totally unaware of their great battle until I broke down on the fifth lap due to a problem with a breather bottle from the tank. A fuel pressure thing. So I stopped at Hillberry having done something like a 118 mph lap and disappointed as I'd gone really well and was on for a superb finish. Obviously it was a mega race because of Steve and Carl but from my own perspective, it's one of those would have, could have, should have been a great result at my first TT. There was a lot of quality in the field as well, Nick Jefferies, Mark Farmer, Iain Duffus people like that.

"I will never forget Steve Hislop on the Padgett's Yamaha passing me at the top of Barregarrow. It was just mind blowing. I didn't really know what happened, he just seemed to suck the paint off the side of my bike as he went past."

JASON GRIFFITHS

More misfortune followed a few weeks later when I broke my collarbone at the Southern 100 but all in all it was a good year. I'd also had solid debuts at the Northwest and Ulster plus my 250 racing around the UK went well enough.

Into 1993 and the TT was a lot different as there was no Hislop or Fogarty but things were the same for me as I had yet another 250 Yamaha and the same RC30 which I would ride for the final time. The Senior went well until I had a misfire which slowed me for the last two laps. That race had been delayed until Saturday morning and we then went straight to Billown for the Post-TT races. I won on the bike even though we hadn't changed anything. We later found out we had a coil breaking down but it coped okay with the short 10 laps, 45 miles race distance, whatever it is around there. Somewhat different to seventy odd miles averaging almost a hundred and twenty miles an hour at the TT for those last two laps which shows how hard the Mountain course can be on a bike.

It was a real team effort at this time. They were Ray's bikes which he was funding while I would be looking after the cost of tyres, things like that. Racing at the TT I liked the Mountain section; it was just so smooth, flowing and open. On the other hand and possibly because of my motocross background I also enjoyed Sulby Bridge to Ramsey. I didn't mind Bray Hill but if you look at it as a sector, I didn't really enjoy the start to Ballacraine too much.

Possibly the closest I came to winning a TT was a race I failed to finish. Well, maybe not win but I was convinced I was going to get a good result in the Junior in 1993. The bike seized and it was all my fault because I jetted it too weak. I wanted to do that. It had been my decision. Beforehand Ray Cowles had said *'no, don't'* but I insisted. I thought I was going to be very competitive but ended up shooting myself in the foot. Brian Reid won and he had Adrian Marsh, who worked closely with Rob McElnea for many years, in his team that day. I can still hear Ady calling me an idiot after I told him the jetting down was my choice.

You're always aware of the dangers at the TT. I'd been around it. I'd done the stuff in Ireland, which was a good grounding. My mentality was it's only dangerous if you crash. You had to ride knowing where the worst bits were for you, where the kerbs were a problem, things like that. The biggest concern in the back of your head was suffering some sort of machine failure or coming across something in the road, whether it be a stricken bike or a cat, things that shouldn't be there. I was confident I wasn't going to cause myself harm but you could never rule out a gearbox seizing or hitting debris, you knew there was always that chance.

I had an early warning of the dangers on one of my first nights as a newcomer practicing for the Manx Grand Prix. I was on the RC 30 coming down Cronk y Voddy straight toward the Eleventh milestone when the guy in front of me suddenly slowed right up. It was clear he had no idea where he was. He slowed that quickly, I couldn't avoid hitting him with my shoulder as I went past. Somehow we both stayed upright. That was pretty scary. Then in the first lap of the Newcomers race my visor fogged up slightly and for a moment I couldn't see where I was going so ran wide into the grass bank close to the 26th milestone which is now known as Joey's. There is a picture somewhere of me on the bike with a bit of shrubbery hanging from the bottom of the left fork leg. This little bit of fogging in the top left hand side of my visor was affecting my concentration so I really had to focus which may have helped me reach 112.56mph on lap two; a Newcomers record. It had really affected me at the time and thankfully we changed the visor at the pitstop

For TT '94 I now had a Kawasaki ZXR-750 plus two of Dennis Trollope's bikes, the Spondon Yamaha 250 and the 660 single. He was in Bristol just across the Severn Bridge from us so we knew him well. He was very, very supportive with an endless enthusiasm for racing, Both of the bikes were bought from Brian Morrison. Ray Cowles seemed to take a step back at this point perhaps because Robert wasn't competing.

Into race week Nigel Davis was leading the Formula One TT when it started to rain which was an experience to say the least. I was on slicks heading down to the bottom of Barregarrow but when I got there the bike suddenly went sideways as the road was absolutely soaked. That was a bit of an eye opener. They soon stopped the race and decided to run it the following day. Unfortunately, I didn't finish the rerun because I had an engine failure approaching Milltown just coming into Ramsey. It was a beautiful sunny afternoon and that's where I met my future wife, Helen. She was marshalling with her brother at Milntown cottage. I stayed at that point for the whole race not just because of the attractive young lady I'd met but the legend was back this year and he was dominating on the new Honda RC45. It was incredible standing there for the entire race watching Steve Hislop go by. He had struggled at the beginning of practice week but seeing the way he rode through a technical part of the circuit was simply a joy. He was visibly faster than the competition; the absolute standout talent of the field.

My Kawasaki was a great bike. I was doing 750 class racing across Britain and had bought two machines from Brian Morrison. He and John Reynolds had been Team Green Kawasaki in '92 when they were the dominant force in British racing and parts like the suspension were from those machines. I'd had a good run at the TT in '94 but beat myself up shortly after when I crashed the 250 at Aberdare Park. We went straight up to Heysham to catch the ferry to the Isle of Man for the Southern 100 road races which started on the Monday. I was still feeling sore in the first practice session but the adrenaline had fully kicked in by Tuesday in the first Superbike race as I finished second to Joey Dunlop who was on the RC45. I won on Wednesday night but Joey had pulled in after a lap or two. Thursday afternoon is the climax of the week at the Southern 100, the championship race and back then it was run over the full 12 laps. Joey had already won the 125cc race around midday when it had been wet and misty. By the time of the big race the rain had stopped but there was still a bit of cloud cover. The track was drying but not ferociously as we went to the warming up area. I hadn't been out, hadn't had a race and it was still damp in places so I put intermediates on the bike. Joey then pulled up alongside me. Everyone knows how Joey wasn't the most talkative of people. I'd previously spent a bit of time with him because of my involvement with Robert so we had a good relationship. As the bikes were idling he leaned across to me and said *"Get those intermediates off and put slicks on"*.

Whereas most people would have said nothing he knew I'd made the wrong decision and wanted to let me know. So I took his advice, after all, he's the great Joey Dunlop and he was right about the conditions. There were a few damp patches here and there but the circuit was dry and we had a mega race, nose to tail for 12 laps. As we came to the final turn at Castletown corner I managed to out-brake him going into teh turn and then held on to the finish line to win by half a bike's length. So his advice had worked against him but he wasn't a bitter man; that wasn't in his nature. I then had a really good Ulster Grand Prix battling with Joey and Phillip McCallen and although I didn't win I came away with the lap record which stood for a little while.

1995 was one of those where you think you've done the right thing but turns out the other way. We sold the Kawasaki '94 bikes, which were a couple of years old and got some help from Kawasaki UK. We built some brand new machinery which had some Kayaba factory suspension plus loads of other special bits but basically it just didn't work out. I struggled my way through the Formula One race and on the last lap, on the approach to Milntown the bracket holding the rear suspension snapped. The back of the bike sat down, I lost all steering and bounced off the wall on the right hand side of the track. I was very lucky because the right hand disc tore off, ripped away the exhaust pipe and footrest while something sliced a hole through my boot cutting my foot open. I didn't actually fall off the bike and managed to stop it. Next it was a chopper ride back to Douglas for an operation on my foot with the knowledge it was the end of my TT for that year. A case of *'what could have been'* as I had a really good 250 from Dennis Trollope and had gone very well on it during practice. The Kawasaki 600 was also good while I really struggled with the big bike all week. Through practice I did a lot of laps on it without getting it to where I wanted and this was playing on my mind. Riding it was a real physical battle and in the race I was counting down the laps thinking *'I've only got to get to the Ramsey and then it's a smooth mountain run'* but that's when it all went wrong. I'm thankful though as it could have been a lot worse.

It didn't put me off the TT, I just found that bike hard to ride. Where I crashed is a real, real fast section but the accident seemed to happen in slow motion. I knew where I was and that there was a wall on the right but what I didn't realise was the road fell away quite a lot into a gulley. I travelled a fair bit along the road so I was lucky the handlebars didn't get tangled up. I leaned it away from the wall but even at that speed I found I had enough time to react and almost think about what I was doing. Your brain seems to process what is happening so quickly yet it doesn't make a lot of sense when you think back. When I came to a stop I thought everything was okay until I felt liquid in my boot as the blood began to fill it.

At that time I was making money out of road racing. It was nothing fantastic but I picked up a few quid at the Northwest and the TT, I did a few small road races, places like Aberdare and a lot of racing at Scarborough. All of the road races were an opportunity to make cash whereas the British championship stuff just cost you money. It was still track time though and I was pursuing what I wanted to do. The year didn't end well either as I had a big crash on the same bike at the Carrowdore 100 in Northern Ireland causing a lot of damage to my right knee. I suffered a lot of ligament damage along with broken bones which meant the leg was in a cast for quite a while. I was finding it quite difficult to bend which meant I had a rethink over the winter about what I was going to do. I spent a lot of time at the Ulster hospital in Dundonald and while I was there I had a call from Bob McMillan who was General Manager of Honda UK with an offer of bikes for next year. He had started as an area rep for South Wales so knew my dad which was a major boost. So I knew I was going into 1996 with some Hondas to ride. Then it was just a question of getting fit which took some time. The fact I couldn't bend my leg properly steered me away from the British championship scene because it was taking me so long to recover. It was easier to ride the road races with their long straights than knee-down short circuits. I did a few but only for track time. From then on it was predominantly the road racing scene.

By now I was making my living from racing. Helen and I married in '96 so I moved to the Isle of Man. I'm aware of the '*best rider never to win a TT'* but I've never given it too much thought. That may have changed had I not crashed in '95 as I had the equipment to do well in the Junior but didn't make the start line. There was the Junior race with the jetting mistake. Another one was in 1999 when I was running really well in a 600 race. It was very tight. We were all very, very close in that one. A valve broke and I lost a lot of revs; David Jefferies went on to win.

Other people make the '*no TT wins*' reference more than I would really. Guy Martin ended up with more podiums than me but then again look how good a rider Roger Marshall was. It's all down to which period you're from I suppose. Roger was probably the most accomplished. He didn't win a TT but lifted British championship titles plus went to Grand Prix and had all sorts of success. For me, you roll the dice. Perhaps I could have tried harder but if I had who knows what would have happened?

My time at the TT is very special to me. I carried on until 2006 after which I called it a day. It was always the highlight of my racing calendar. When we did the morning practices and if it was the last one on a Friday, maybe some riders had had a good practice week, maybe people thought the weather was gonna be bad so there'd be a possibility you wouldn't have many competitors out at all. So you'd set off on a cracking Manx morning at quarter past five, do two laps of the TT course and maybe not see another bike; you felt like you'd got the best proving ground all for yourself. Pure magic.

It was all an experience. Some of the stuff riding in Ireland will stay with me forever. Tandragee in 1991 with Robert especially. Setting off in convoy with Joey having left the race meeting and stopping at the Way-side Halt on the way back. Having a few beers with everybody while a few of the guys were singing. Special times.

Jason brought his racing to an end while he was still at the top of his game in 2006. He opened up his own business Jason Griffiths Motorcycles in the Isle of Man and co-ordinates Pirelli Tyres Ltd's involvement in the British Superbike championship. He and wife Helen have four daughters.

DAVE LEACH

Born Halifax, England

TT Years 1985-1991,1995, 1997
4 x wins, 2 x 2nd, 1 x 3rd, 2 x 4th, 2 x 5th, 3 x 6th, 1 x 7th, 3 x 8th, 2 x 9th, 3 x 10th, 2 x 11th, 1 x 13th, 1 x 14th, 2 x 16th, 2 x 19th, 1 x 20th, 1 x 22nd, 1 x 24th, 1 x 29th, 1 x 68th, 6 x DNF

MGP Years 1982-84
2 x 4th, 1 x 5th, 1 x 6th, 1 x 9th, 3 x DNF

The record books may have Dave Leach as a four-time TT winner but it could be argued he actually has six. A solid rider with a solid record, incredibly failing to finish just six of the forty-two TTs he took part in during an era when reliability issues could see half the entry list fail to make it to the chequered flag. He gelled with Production machinery better than most around the Mountain course and his battles with rivals Carl Fogarty and Steve Hislop are embedded in TT folklore yet while they went on to British and World Superbike title triumphs Dave's career went in a different direction. Like so many in a sport of incredible highs and lows it was a near-death crash which brought everything to a premature end despite a comeback of sorts a few years later.

I was introduced to bikes at an early age as my Dad used to go scrambling. He was quite good, competing at county level plus he also owned road bikes and would often make the journey to the Isle of Man each year to watch the TT. My first trip to the Island was in 1973 when Phil Haslam rode the first 100 mile-an-hour Manx Grand Prix lap on his way to winning the Junior. It was a family holiday for ten-year-old me with my parents and sister and we stayed at the Melrose boarding house in Douglas which was our regular digs in the early years. Mal Carter lived a few miles away from us in Barkisland near Halifax and he was sponsoring Phil so when he won, it was big news back home in the village. The following year I came with my Dad for my first of many TT visits on the back of his bike and was there for Mike Hailwood's return, Phil Read's comeback and Joey Dunlop's early days.

1978 was something special although things didn't start too well as we lost the bag containing our clothes when it came loose as we crossed the M62 on dad's bike. Jamie Whitham came with us as well for his first trip to the TT. His dad and mine were good friends but there was no room for them at the Melrose so they stayed at a private house nearby. The Island was absolutely heaving and all because of the return of Hailwood. Folk think it's busy now yet I'd say there were ten times more people over that year. We watched the race at Hillberry and you could hear the roar from the Grandstand when Mike went over the line. It made the hairs on the back of your neck stand up; it was unbelievable.

Jamie's dad had the Crosland Moor airfield near Huddersfield so we used to test bikes up and down the runway. I'd just started racing and James would sometimes come with us and even though he was only something like twelve-years-old you could see he was itching to have a go. He got his chance when his dad bought him a 125 from Steve Crowther, a good friend of mine, who'd raced in the Honda series. James came along with me to Carnaby as I was competing there and took part in his first race meeting.

As I passed into my teenage years, I'd begun doing trials, the sport was big in Yorkshire and I did quite well in the youth class but eventually started to drift away. I wanted to go racing and in 1981 Steve Crowther told me about the new 350 LC Yamaha that was coming out. I knew right away I wanted it so we both ended up buying one. We rode them on the road to run them in but he had a very bad accident on his, smashing it to bits, hurting himself in the process. He recovered and so did the bike with Steve making a bit of a special out of it, turning it into a F2 outfit. Toward the end of the year I started production racing and then in 1982 I did my first full season, organised by the Auto 66 Club, racing at places like Carnaby, Elvington and Cadwell Park plus I also made my Manx Grand Prix debut.

The bike I would ride over the Mountain course was a Yamaha TZ250 G which had been ridden by Alan Carter. His father Mal said it was perfect for the Isle of Man so my father bought it from him. Dad was keen for me to do the Manx. I took the bike to the Isle of Man in a transit van but didn't have the luxury of a garage so worked on it at the front of the Melrose where we were staying once more. It wasn't the greatest of years to be making a debut as it was wet most of the time especially during practice. As I'd been going there for years I more or less knew my way around the circuit but now the road was twice as wide plus I was going twice as fast than I'd been used to so it was certainly a memorable experience and a quite scary one, if I'm honest. I was riding at speeds I'd never reached before; the fastest I'd been at that time was probably down the straight at Cadwell Park or around the roads near my home when testing bikes. On the TT course and because of the speed I was now going, the corners were sometimes coming up too quickly so you really had to think where you were on the racetrack as you could easily forget. Once I had a few laps under my belt I felt okay even though there were a lot of wet practice sessions plus mist on the mountain yet they never stopped for rain or poor visibility in those days. I enjoyed it though and went on to finish fourth and fifth in both races.

I came close to winning in 1984 which was my third year at the Manx. I was leading the Junior race until I slid off at Signpost on the second lap. I remounted and made my way back to the pits where we had to take off the bottom half of the fairing which became something of a regular feature for me at the TT. I went on to finish in sixth place, Ian Newton won it but my last lap was faster than anybody else's so at least that was something of a bonus. After the race we noticed we had totally the wrong compound tyre on the bike; it was too hard. The person who sold it to me insisted it was the rubber we needed. I suppose you learn from your mistakes. Having had three goes at the Manx it seemed I was never going to win it so decided it was time to move on to the TT. The year ended on a high when I won the Marlboro British Clubmans championship.

I was riding a lot on the roads near my home and they were very similar to those in the Isle of Man so perhaps that could explain why I seemed to do well in the Production classes. When I got to the TT I was getting a fair bit of support from sponsors, Ian Booth of local firm Westvale Engineering helped get me a Kawasaki GPZ900, Shell Oils stepped in along with Transcast who later became Swedish Truck Parts. I'd started racing in Ireland at this point and I was getting good results at a lot of places like the Ulster Grand Prix. I came sixth in the big bike Proddie race on my TT debut and the following year took my first win at the TT. In 1986 I crossed the line in seventh position in the Senior but that year the 250s were part of the race and I was the leading rider in that category so was classified as the winner. If you look at the trophy you'll see my name's on it although I didn't find this out until sometime later. The 350s were dying off but the 250 class was still strong and therefore the machines were being swapped around a bit. I was on a 250 Yamaha with Hummel 320 cylinders on it, the bloody thing was flying. In the Junior TT I was level with Steve Cull on time at the Bungalow and as I came out of Signpost the bike burbled a bit and I thought *'oh shit!'* My fears came true as I went into the dip at Governors Bridge and the fuel dried up so I ended up pushing the bike home to claim fourth.

It was also the race when Gene McDonnell tragically lost his life at Ballaugh. It happened not long before I got there and when I arrived, I was going that fast you couldn't tell what had occurred, no sooner were you over the bridge you were on your way. I thought *'Bloody hell, what was that?'* You just couldn't believe what you'd seen. There were no flags out so I assumed it couldn't have been that bad. It wasn't until after the race I found out he'd struck a horse that had strayed onto the track.

In the Production B race I rode my Dad's Honda VFR750 and I was going quite well until it started to drizzle. I thought about how he'd react if I pushed and ended up dropping it so I eased off to eventually finish fifth but when I got back he gave me a bollocking for slowing down. To my surprise, I got home to a letter from Honda Britain congratulating me on doing so well on that bike.

Over the winter I'd agreed to ride for Padgett's in 1987. The deal gave me the opportunity to ride better machinery. Peter Padgett offered me the Suzuki RG500 plus the chance to ride in the European 500cc championship and, at the time, you could also try to qualify for the World Grand Prix series. Anybody could back then and that was the road I wanted to go down. Those plans were scuppered though when I crashed at Greeba Castle in the TT and broke my leg. That year I was supposed to be riding the Suzuki F1 bike at the start of the week in the Formula One race but we just couldn't get it to perform how we wanted it to. I'd struggled with it all week through practice then Peter said he had something in the back of the van I could ride instead; this was the night before the race. I was fearing the worst until they brought out this 750 Suzuki Canadian spec full-on production bike but it had a dry clutch. It looked something special so I decided to give it a go, put some decent tyres on and get it prepared. I'd be surprised if you can do that nowadays to race a machine you'd not thrown your leg over. The plan was if it was still going in a straight line by the time I reached the bottom of Bray Hill then that would do. Thankfully, it did. I ended up having a good ride on it and finished eighth which was amazing on a production bike so it was a good decision to swap. The rest of the classes were looking good. I had one of Gary Padgett's Honda 250s which he'd ridden before as well as his ex-Formula Two machine which was a missile. Midway through the Junior race I was sitting in the top six when a few spots of rain began to appear. I'd just come over the brow on the right hand bend at Greeba when the bike tucked under and I went straight into the wall. I broke my femur so that was me out for most of the season although I did come

"As I went through Whitebridges the bike went completely sideways and tried to pitch me off so from there I just short-shifted, trying not to make any silly moves. Luckily it held on until the end so it was a mixture of joy and relief as I took the chequered flag."

DAVE LEACH

and tried a few meetings in Ireland at the end of the racing year. By this time I was used to competing every weekend, there was always a meeting going on somewhere which meant you could earn some good cash. I was now being paid by organisers for starting races and the Padgett deal was that we'd agreed to split start and prize money 50/50 down the middle. It wasn't that bad an arrangement as they were supplying the bikes while I funded the tyres and other running costs so it did work out quite well.

I stayed with Padgett's for another season with a similar deal, competing in Europe plus the odd Grand Prix and did the British round that year. Peter said they'd get me a bike for the TT which turned out to be the Bimota who were having a big push with Mitsui Yamaha bringing them in. Geoff Johnson also rode one. I finished the Formula One TT in ninth.

The Production Class A race was a different affair. I was leading on the Yamaha FZR1000 when the chain began jumping off the sprocket as I went up the Gooseneck on the final lap. Throughout the race I'd been holding my own with a five to six second lead but as I began the climb toward the Mountain it seemed my efforts would be in vain and what made it worse was it would be my fault as I'd gone for a non-o-ring chain for less drag. It looked like a big mistake. As I went through Whitebridges the bike went completely sideways and tried to pitch me off so from there I just short-shifted, trying not to make any silly moves. Luckily it held on until the end so it was a mixture of joy and relief as I took the chequered flag. I was guided into the winning enclosure to be told I'd won but I didn't know how close it was until they announced over the speakers I'd done it by eight tenths of a second over Geoff Johnson. Meanwhile the chain was hanging off so it was a close call on both counts. To stand on the top step of a TT podium does get to you, it is a bit emotional when you go up onto the rostrum and they play the national anthem. It felt good though.

The big production bikes back then had a fearsome reputation at the TT but I never seemed to have any problems with them apart from the odd moment. There were quite a few Proddie racing specialists around, Geoff Johnson, Brian Morrison, people like that and I seemed to gel with the production bikes at the TT rather than full-on racing machines. Both Jamie Whitham and his team-mate Phil Mellor said they had awful problems trying to get the Suzuki to go in a straight line around the Isle of Man. I found that weird because I'd ridden with Mez at Snetterton in a six-hour race when we teamed up on a Suzuki 1100 and it was brilliant on a short circuit. They were good, better than the Yamaha but on the road circuit they just didn't handle. I'd battled with Jamie when he rode the 1100 at the NorthWest 200 and we were together all around the circuit. He dived inside me at Church corner after I nearly high sided, so it showed the Suzuki was good there. Perhaps the TT course was just too bumpy. It rained for the last big race at the NorthWest that year so a few of us went out on production bikes and we were right up there in the top six, in fact Jamie led it for a little while. They were missiles in a straight line.

Andy Smith from Yamaha was on the phone at the end of the year offering a deal but I didn't want to upset Padgett's. Mark Phillips, who had ridden for Padgetts a few years earlier, and was a Yamaha rider, persuaded me to take the ride so that's what happened, I left on good terms and Padgett's never held it against me.

I also had a bit of a sniff from Honda after I rode the Padgett's RC30 at Kirkistown. Darren Dixon was due to ride it but was injured so Clive suggested I give it a go, which I did and it was brilliant; I wish I'd ridden that at the TT! There were other offers but the smart money was on Yamaha so I went to see Andy Smith. It wasn't a full-on works deal like Terry Rymer had at the time but they would give me the bikes and I would run my own team with my own sponsors. Jack Valentine and Steve Mellor at V&M were starting to help me as well so along with some good support from people like Jim Watters in Ireland we put a good package together.

Yamaha had a new model for 1989, the FZR1000 Exup so they wanted to show how good it was by winning the Production TT, which we did. All the newspapers carried big adverts on the back of it, which goes to show how important it was to them. On the downside it was the race in which Steve Henshaw and Phil Mellor lost their lives. When I returned to the TT later in my career I'd often think '*Bloody hell, am I right doing this? There's going to be people not coming back on this ferry*' but it never really sticks in your mind when you're younger even though it's happening around you. There was one particular year in Ireland when it seemed like someone was being killed every week, Sam McClements was one of them, it was horrendous. Somehow, you sort of put it all to one side.

There was one time I wasn't going to race and that was when Phil Hogg died during practice. I was staying at Norley House in Douglas which was run by his parents, Alex and Sheila, and I told them of my decision but they insisted I went ahead as that is what Phil would have wanted.

One race people do remember is the battle I had with Carl Fogarty and Steve Hislop in the Production 750 TT in 1989. Foggy did two steady laps before pitting while Hizzy came in at the end of the first which meant we were all together on road for the last lap as Steve had started ten seconds ahead of me and Carl. They were Honda team-mates so Hizzy would try and slow me down to let Foggy get away but I wasn't having any of it. My biggest concern though was the exhaust bracket hanging from my silencer which I thought I'd be black flagged for but thankfully wasn't. We swapped positions a few times from the Bungalow as we headed towards the finish line. There's a picture of Carl and myself at the 33rd milestone and we're both side by side around the bank, more or less leaning in on one another. I then got him going into the Creg but he then did the same to me at Brandish. We were level going into Hillberry but I was on the inside so realised I had to let him go. As we got to Governors I was going to go for it but thought against it as I was afraid we would end up in a heap if I did. So Foggy went on to win what would be his first TT victory.

My second TT win came in the 400 and it was a brilliant race. There's TV footage of this one where there's five or six of us all together on the road. I'd set off 10 seconds behind Carl and had caught him. I drew level with him coming out of the Creg and down towards Brandish so when

I went past I looked over at him and waved! He would have wanted to cross the line first even though I had 10 seconds on him but I wasn't going to give him that small pleasure. I always got on well with Carl even though he was fairly quiet back then. We always speak when we meet as we'd raced each other for years. He was a hard rider though, he would never give you an inch. If we were on equal machinery at the TT we could give each other a battle, there was never much in it. You could say the same about Steve Hislop but there was one difference with him; no matter what the bikes, if he was on it and everything was right then he was untouchable. He was that good. After the race there were a lot of rumours going around that I had a big engine because you could bore them out to 480 but there was no way we'd have risked that. It was stripped afterwards and everything was legal.

I was promised a certain amount of money for starting the TT one year but when I picked up my brown envelope it was only half of what we'd agreed. So I asked the bloke who'd given it to me what was going on and he said I had to go see Jim Parker who was the Chairman of the ACU. When I did he was adamant that it was all I was going to get however, when I'd picked up my cheque I saw the sheet with everyone's name on it and how much they were being paid. That had me fuming so I kept on at Jim through practice week but he refused to budge until it came to the start of one of the big Production races. I threatened that if I won I wouldn't stand on the rostrum but instead would go straight to the press centre and explain the reason why I'd refused to go up. I simply wasn't happy about the manner in which I was being treated. Jim came to me five minutes before the start of the race, when I was on the start grid and told me he would sort it out. About an hour after the garlanding ceremony I went to the ACU office to find the rest of my money was there.

I eventually fell out with the ACU over the grading lists for the TT Formula One World championship rounds. I'd put myself forward and like every federation, they have to guarantee their top four or five riders a start for practice but not the race. The list came out and I'm down in something like tenth while there were others above me in the order who were only going to do a couple of rounds. I knew one of the teams had put their riders on it yet I knew damn well they weren't doing all of the series. I rang the ACU to find out why they'd done this and they argued as it was a works team they wanted to guarantee them a ride. I was pals with Roger Marshall who was riding for Suzuki at the time and he suggested I get an Irish licence as I was doing a lot of riding in Ireland. So I contacted the MCUI who sent me a form to fill in, which I did and I told them I wanted to go on the grading list for the TT F1 rounds. They said Joey and Robert Dunlop were first and second so would I be happy at third? You bet! This was great, I was guaranteed a start. I didnt want a repeat of the time when I went all the way to Misano in Italy for one of the rounds and didn't even get to go out. There'd been a free practice session on the Wednesday before the event and I'd been something like fourth quickest but because I was number eleven on the list the organisers wouldn't allow me a start in practice. We'd gone all that way for nothing, I was gutted. So it was important for me to have a high grading and that's why I switched my ACU licence for one with the MCUI.

I had a very good sponsor in Ireland and that was because I was doing the Irish roads plus I was making a living out of it, paying the bills with the guarantee of good rides with good start money in places. When Steve Hislop was first racing his Formula 2 bike he was sleeping in the back of his van when he came to Ireland so my sponsor Jim insisted he stayed with us in his house. That's when Hizzy and I became good mates.

Going to race full time in Ireland was probably the biggest mistake careerwise I ever made even though I enjoyed it and made loads of friends, many I still have today. Perhaps I should have followed Foggy and Hizzy by racing in the UK instead. Jamie Whitham has always insisted I should have done the British championship but the truth is I couldn't afford to do it. He was going well at the time having just got his ride with Mick Grant while I went the other way. It was a tough decision for me. When I rode for Padgett's in the European 500 championship in 1988 I'd had some good results, lots of top ten finishes including a second place at Le Mans. I became friendly with an Italian lad who had a couple of the Honda

3-cylinders, his family was absolutely loaded and he was selling one at the end of the year. I wanted to buy it but he wanted something like 25 grand which was a lot of money at the time. I mentioned it to Clive Padgett but he insisted they were sticking with Suzuki. I can't help thinking that if he had bought it, then I probably would have raced in the UK. I also approached a few of my sponsors and borrowed everything I could but I just couldn't raise the money; it just wasn't to be. If I had then I would definitely have raced another year in the European 500s which could have led onto a Grand Prix career. I knew I still had the ability to ride short circuits because I did the European 600 series when it ran alongside World Superbike in 1991. It looked as if I would win that title until I had a DNF at Misano and I lost out on the championship by one point at Monza in the last round. That could have been the start of something else as well but I've no regrets as I had some good times in Ireland. I was still racing at Daytona and lots of European circuits like Salzburg, Assen, Hockenheim, Jerez, Hungaroring, Vila Real and Kouvola in Finland.

I had a similar deal to race Yamahas in 1990. It was another great package with V&M doing all the motors. I went to Daytona that year, came fourth in the 600 race and something like seventh or eighth in the 200 miler, so the season started very well and continued that way with some good results in Ireland. This was also the last year of the TT F1 championship due to the emergence of World Superbikes which had started up in 1988. I rode in the first ever WSB round at Donington which you had to qualify for. There were so many riders that had turned up for practice we had to be split into two groups. I managed to qualify and finished fifteenth in the first ever World Superbike race and thirteenth in the second. From then on I competed when I could in both series as there was good money on offer. Anybody finishing in the top 15 in TTF1 was offered an entry into the next round of World Superbikes and roughly 2000 Swiss francs. It was a way of keeping top riders in both events. The way the calendar worked, the rounds rolled on the week after each other in Europe so you could go abroad for three or four months and earn a bit of money while you were out there. The TT Formula One championship was strong with the likes of Carl Fogarty, Phillip McCallen and Joey Dunlop taking part. I had a great race at Dundrod which Joey won ahead of Robert and I was third but I had the fastest lap. It was one of those days where it was damp then dry, damp again then dry again. Typical Ulster Grand Prix weather!

Yamaha were celebrating thirty years of racing in 1991 and they'd brought one of their World Endurance 750 bikes for me to ride at the TT. Rob McElnea was the team boss, Brian Morrison was my team-mate and he was sticking with his standard 0W machine while I still had mine so brought that with me too. The first time I rode the 750 was at Jurby which is a one-time airstrip in the north of the Isle of Man and I couldn't believe how quick the bike was. It had a sort of overdrive in top gear where it just pulled and pulled and kept on pulling. We had two Japanese mechanics in the team and even though they could speak very little English they understood what I meant when I came in after 20 minutes to tell them how fast this was when they saw the huge smile on my face. Even though Honda were at the TT with the all-conquering RVFs I thought I was in with a shout on this bike. I took it easy on the first night of practice as I wanted to get used to it because down the straights it was probably one of the fastest bikes out there. However, it didn't handle the bumps too well from Ginger Hall through to Ramsey but I was confident we could sort it. On Thursday afternoon practice I'd set off around ten seconds in front of Steve Hislop and he caught and passed me on that very section where I'd been struggling so I then stuck him with him all the way up the Mountain. We were together coming out of the Bungalow but I pulled out and zipped away from him. When we got back he said he couldn't believe how fast my bike was so I pointed out he must have noticed how I'd been struggling to handle it properly from Ginger Hall. No matter what we did we just couldn't get the bike right and we were running out of time so I suggested we take the engine out and put it into my chassis as I had kit forks and swinging arm but a standard frame. The Japanese guys were keen to do it but for some reason Rob didn't want to know. He wanted the bike like that on the line and I knew damn well if I pushed too hard it would throw me off. My screen also broke as it was being cleaned during the pitstop so half of it was missing for the last two laps. I wasn't happy.

I stuck with Yamaha for 1992 and got the year underway with my annual pilgrimage to Daytona followed by the Irish races and the Regal 600 which had some super-fast men in it like Brian Reid, Leslie McMaster, Philip McCallen and Steve Cull to name but a few. Half of the rounds were on roads and the first three were on short circuits. Tandragee was the opening road race that year instead of Cookstown and I was leading the championship when we got there. I even rode to victory in the classic race that weekend on a G50 that belonged to Gordon Bell. By the start of the 600 race it had started to rain but the problem was we could only ride on road tyres as we weren't allowed to put wets on. There was a lot of discussion beforehand but we decided to go for it. The rain was really coming down as we got underway and there was that much water on the track we were aquaplaning everywhere. I was on the second lap and coming over the brow just before Bell's Crossroads when the bike went sideways. There seemed to be some ruts in the road so it was as if I was stuck in a tram line which pulled me straight into the ditch and down I went. They put me in an ambulance and I was conscious on the way to the hospital but then it would be about a month until I knew where I was.

I'd snapped my pelvis and it now had a six inch gap down the middle. I'd broken both legs as well as my ankles plus suffered a lot of internal injuries including a collapsed lung. I was told they put about 40 pints of blood through my body to keep me going. I was on life support for a long time. If it hadn't been for the staff at Belfast City Hospital I don't think I'd be alive today. When I came out of it and started to recover I just wanted to get back on a bike again, there was no thought of quitting; racing was all I knew. I needed something to be positive to keep me going, I just kept saying to myself *'I'm going to race again, I'm going to race again'*. My right leg became infected and I might have lost it had they not removed a muscle out of the bottom of it. It was weeks before I was anywhere near sitting up in bed. I was then transferred back to Yorkshire to be near my family and spent time in two hospitals there as I recuperated. Eventually I was well enough to leave and this was about a week before the Manx Grand Prix so I travelled over to the Isle of Man to watch the races; I shouldn't have done but I did.

As I recovered it meant 1993 was a washout but all the time I kept thinking I had to find something and eventually I did in the shape of the Harley Davidson 883 series. I could manage that because you more or less keep them in the same gear to ride around. I was struggling with movement in my ankles and really shouldn't have been riding at all as I had to be lifted on and off. So I did that series and had a few good results in some of the races. Next I was back on my 400 so I started racing again and came back to the TT in 1995 although I knew in the back of my mind my legs weren't strong enough. When you ride around the Isle of Man you do so more with your legs than your arms. You're pushing all the time from your feet upwards and standing on the foot rests. I had some decent results but also one or two big moments which made me come to my senses. I realised I was going the other way now, just riding for the fun of it, not to win. My best result during my comeback was as runner-up to Jason Griffiths at the Southern 100 on my Supersport bike. It had just started to rain which slowed the pace down. I did score another TT win of sorts when I finished as the top 400 rider in the 250 race.

In 1997 I was to ride a Triumph 595 in the TT Production race. The British manufacturer had just made their comeback and this was something I was really keen to get involved with.

Things didn't start too well at the NorthWest 200 when the exhaust dropped to bits; it was also slow and not handling too well. We took it back to Yorkshire where my mechanic Alan spotted the frame had broken. With the TT days away time was tight and after some to-ing and fro-ing Triumph supplied a new one. We worked around the clock and managed to get it ready by the time we left for the Island.

On the Wednesday evening practice session, I was lucky to keep control of the bike when the handlebar came loose as I went through Greeba Bridge. I exited the track at Ballacraine and rode back on the road to the Grandstand to get back out on another bike. A close inspection of the Triumph showed the handlebar had been machined wrong which caused it to work its way loose. I was due to get married at the end of TT week and things were just not sitting right with one problem after another so I decided the idea of the Triumph ride wasn't worth the risk. My bride-to-be Becky contacted Dave Goodley who brought over one of Nick Morgan's bikes for me to ride in the Production race. I bumped into the TT commentator Fred Clarke that evening, who I have known since the Marlboro Clubman days, and we chatted about what had happened with the Triumph in the practice session. I asked him if he could make an announcement on my behalf during the Thursday afternoon practice session, which he did. I'd decided I would retire from racing. I just didn't want to risk it anymore. It was to be my final season.

My last ever meeting was the Gold Cup at Scarborough that same year. It was a good place to finish my career as I'd raced at Oliver's Mount for a long time and enjoyed some good results. Some people are not too fond of the late Peter Hillaby but he always looked after me, I got on well with him. When I won the Marlboro Clubmans he gave me an envelope with 500 quid in it and told me to put it to good use. He always took care of me at any of the big meetings. I think he looked out for all those who came through the club, riders like Dave Dean and Phil Mellor, Jamie Whitham was another and like a lot of good racers, plied their trade at Carnaby and Elvington. I'd started off with the Auto 66 Club, which Peter was in charge of, so it was nice to finish there too.

My racing fix then came via a touring bike. Becky and I used to go abroad to watch Grand Prix and World Superbikes at tracks like Brno, Misano, all the usual haunts. I'd made good friends in Italy so we would visit them. We used to go and watch sidecar motocross too, we got right into that, it was good fun. Eventually we moved to the Isle of Man, not through any connection with the TT but because we'd found a business to buy so settled down here. Strangely, being the Isle of Man, I sold the road bike and now my only journeys over the Mountain course are by car to and from work. Whenever the question of my TT wins comes up I always insist I won '*four and six!*'

When he packed up racing Dave worked for a family firm in Yorkshire but eventually he and wife Becky moved to the Isle of Man where they still live with their son to run their own packaging business. Dave is involved with the local off-road scene and helps organise events in the Island as a member of the Ramsey Motorcycle Club including bringing rounds of the British Enduro Championship as well as being the man behind the Circuit of Mann All-Terrain Rally.

ROB MCELNEA

Born Scunthorpe, England

TT Years 1982-84
7 races, 3 wins, 1 x 3rd, 3 x DNF

MGP 1979, 1981
3 races, 1 x 2nd, 2 x DNF

Rob McElnea was the last of the TT superstars to go on to become a World Grand Prix championship rider. In a brief period at the Isle of Man in the early 1980s he raced seven times, winning on three occasions, grabbing a third place and failing to finish the other three. He also left the Island as the outright lap record holder at over 118mph. HIs was a brief but successful time at the TT but unlike John Surtees and Giacomo Agostini who have similar records to Rob and of whom both it could be argued never really regularly came up against quality opposition to match their talent the same cannot be said of McElnea. He triumphed in a field containing the likes of Mick Grant, Roger Marshall, Charlie Williams, Tony Rutter, Brian Reid, all multiple TT winners while it will be his titanic battles with Joey Dunlop that will be remembered forever by those who witnessed them. Rob would return to the TT as a team manager taking care of Carl Fogarty in the classic battle of 1992 featuring Steve Hislop and the Norton. Plus he

had a parade lap ride to forget during the centenary celebrations in 2007.

My Dad came from Southern Ireland and he raced in the late '50s, early '60s at a reasonably good level. He then stopped to concentrate on running his business but started racing again around 1972, just on the club circuits at national level and as a youngster I was dragged along with the circus. So at a very early age I'd been introduced to racing. He was a short circuit man, never racing the roads. When I first started we both raced together at the same events for a year or so. I was on a 400 Honda but while he also had a Honda his was an 850. So I used to get the hole-shot but he had the power so he would soon fly past me. We'd have a bit of a dice and then I'd shit myself as I was racing against my Dad. The outcome of a race could make for interesting conversations on the journey home.

He used to take me to the Isle of Man to watch the TT even though he never raced there. I was there in 1975, sat with my dad on the bank just before Governors Bridge when Mick Grant smashed Mike Hailwood's eight-year-old lap record. He was riding the three-cylinder Kawasaki in the Classic but failed to finish the six-lapper when his chain broke halfway through the race allowing John Williams to go on to win. Sat there waiting for Granty to appear is a vivid memory. I seem to remember Tony Rutter's chain coming off at Ballaugh in the same race when he was leading on lap five.

I was never that desperate to be a TT rider. I loved my time going there as a fan but when i started racing I was just scratching around short circuits. I carried on like that for most of my career, I sort of never had a plan; it all just fell into place. A pal of mine did the Manx Grand Prix one year on his 250 and he loved it. He recommended I do it as I was just getting going on my TZ. So I went on to do the Manx and totally loved it. I was hooked.

Back then the Newcomers was a big grid and was a separate race. I remember feeling quite worried filling in the entry form. You're extremely nervous writing it out in January or whenever it was, really shitting yourself as you put a stamp on it and by the time you've reached the post box things are really fucking scary! Then you put it in the slot and it's like *'oh fuck, what am I doing?'* Then you're just waiting for a reply. A lot of people didn't get in but I managed to at the first attempt. I received my confirmation, got my number; I would be 42. Then it became this massive thing to look forward to, counting down the months.

When the time came I travelled to the Island with my mate who had done the Manx before. We were working together out of his garage in Scunthorpe. I had a Marina pickup in which I put my TZ350 on one side of the back, the RD250 on the other and every single thing I owned to go racing with jammed in the middle. My girlfriend was with me as we set off for the Isle of Man. You should have seen us. A proper travelling gypsy-type set up. I had so much weight on the back of this little Marina as we cruised along the M62 in the pissing rain going to the ferry, the rubber on the tyres millimetres away from the wheel arches. At the time I was fairly skint, boosted by a bit of sponsorship to help me buy the bike with everything else just sort of cobbled together with whatever money I could get my hands on.

Nothing prepares you for your first time setting off down towards Bray Hill. It was early morning practice. I'd gone out on the RD in normal everyday traffic, just riding around and around the track, all day long whenever I could but nothing gets you ready for that first time when you let the clutch out on the 350 to go flat out along Glencrutchery road at five o'clock in the morning. Yet it was such a buzz. What an adventure! We stayed in the Rio hotel on Douglas seafront or the R 10 as it was affectionately known by the Irish contingent. We worked out the back of Mylchreests garage. There were loads of us in there. The camaraderie between everyone, especially the Irish was just absolutely brilliant. It was incredible, getting up at four in the morning, going to do a couple of hours practice and then back to the hotel for a full monty breakfast.

I was a really quick learner of circuits. I think a lot of it was because I was so big and learning my trade at Cadwell Park, which was my local track. If I didn't work out the layouts, I just couldn't go fast, simple as that.

If you weren't smart and disciplined enough to learn tracks you'd struggle. Being a heavy bloke, if I couldn't carry momentum to get through the turn and get a good exit out of the corner then I was goosed. At the Isle of Man if you mess up the entry you won't have a good exit which is crucial as there are many long straights therefore I was very disciplined in my learning. Thankfully, I was pretty sharp on the short circuits due to being so focused which helped me learn the TT course quite quickly. There were still parts of the Mountain course which I could never get quite right even by the time I finished racing there while there are certain sections you have to treat with so much respect that you learn them like the back of your hand. I soon worked out it wasn't the sort of place to try and scratch your bollocks off especially around places like Creg ny Baa. You don't make time up there. It's all about the fast flowing fourth, fifth gear parts of the track where you've got to keep yourself moving. It doesn't really matter too much about being a heavy guy at the TT because it just flows. Even though I clicked with it and was pretty fast straight away I never really got that cocky around there. In practice I tried to be fast all the time. Then come race day I really got my head down.

The Manx Grand Prix Newcomers race of 1979 was over four laps. I had my mate in the pits and everything was going to plan especially with an advantage of half a minute over second place coming out of Ramsey for the last time. I was already thinking

'*Christ, a thirty second lead going over the Mountain. I've done all the hard work. I've just got to cruise across Snaefell and I've won the Manx Newcomers!*'.

I'd just had my board at Ramsey telling me about the size of my lead when, two hundred yards later, I bloody fall off. It's a memory that will never leave me. I was coming into White Gates which was like a washboard, the surface full of ripples but you just wobbled through it lap after lap. This time though the front folded and down I went. I chased the bike, managing to pick it up while it was still sliding along the road and jumped back on again. Everything on the bike looked pretty straight, no sign of damage. Perhaps I could have probably ridden harder over the

"I'd just had my board at Ramsey telling me about the size of my lead when, two hundred yards later, I bloody fall off. It's a memory that will never leave me."

ROB MCELNEA

Mountain but I still thought I was alright and had done enough to win. Yet I ended up losing by two seconds to Roger Luckman. I probably lost time getting my head back into it. When I got going again it took me until I was past the Gooseneck before I had settled in once more.

I skipped a year at the Manx but returned in 1981 on my 750, treaded tyres and all. I was doing well until my inner tube disintegrated. So I never finished that one. My TT debut came in '82, again on the Yamaha but I failed to finish both races. In one of them, the weather was horrible, very dodgy. I was so psyched out with everything that I forgot about my fuel stop and ran out of juice at Kirk Michael on lap three.

By 1983 I had a bit of a plan in so much that I wanted to go as far as I could on the short circuits and in the World Championship Grand Prix. That became the goal even though I never set it out to be, I never chased a championship, never looked for anything in terms of setting targets, just wanted to find out what I was capable of achieving. The way the Suzuki ride came about was a bit of a weird one. At the end of '82, I'd had a good season and I was talking to Honda team boss Barry Symmons. We were close to agreeing a deal but at the last minute they signed Roger Marshall from Suzuki. He'd just won the British championship for the third time, pipping Wayne Gardner to the title, offering him a load of dollars so he left Suzuki which opened the door there for me. It probably could have gone either way. Both of them were interested in me, mainly for the roads more than the short circuits to be fair because at that time the TT was such a big thing. So the Suzuki deal was there for me and obviously doing the TT is in the contract along with the Formula One World Championship. I was nervous as well as really excited because I'd been at the Isle of Man as a MGP rider plus done the odd TT and seen all the factory teams in the plush hotels. The Suzuki bosses would stay in an old house close to Braddan Bridge with the riders at the Castle Mona Hotel on Douglas sea front. I used to walk past, see them all in their matching jackets, somewhat in awe thinking, *'wow, look at that factory team'*. Now it was me wearing the same gear as Mick Grant. We'd go out to the HQ at the big house. Everybody would be there. The team bus sat outside and I'm now going '*bloody hell I'm one of the factory boys*.' It was all a bit surreal.

The fans were great. Always encouraging you, asking for autographs as everyone did back then. The attention was nice but really it was all about you focusing on the racing. You're in the big time now. everybody's looking at you, watching everything and you're expected to do the business. I was Mick Grant's understudy. So that was a little bit of pressure off me because he was the TT man. I'd been much quicker than him all around short circuits leading up to there. I guess I was still fairly new at the TT and not as familiar with the course as Mick, still with quite a lot to learn.

There was always plenty going on, the whole Island would be buzzing but I never really went out too much. We did lots of things with the likes of Ted McCauley of the Daily Mirror, loads of promotional stuff throughout the week. By '84 having won one, things became much busier for me especially as I was expected to win again

I didn't mix too much with the other riders, you tended to stay with your team in your own little bubble. Even though I raced against him I never really knew Joey very well especially to talk to. Roger Marshall was a good mate of mine plus Mick of course but I just pretty much did my own thing. You'd do your debrief with the team and talk to your team-mate but rarely socialised together unlike my Manx Grand Prix days. That was more like a gang of guys having a great time, sitting in the garage together and just talking bollocks all day. It would often begin with how you survived your morning practice, things like that, the camaraderie was brilliant. As soon as you step into the factory team, things really change. You tended not to share too much info at this level. All through my career I never really had that many racing mates so I didn't spend that much time with other riders.

By 1983 my parents were living in Bahrain. Mum came over to watch me race the TT that year but Dad didn't, he stayed in the Middle East. So he missed my first TT win and the big party at the Rio that night to celebrate. It was the place to be, so much fun, mixing with a gang of Irish guys. The hotel had looked after me so well during my time at the Manx that I stayed there again when I raced at the TT. Someone I hadn't expected to see that night though was the police.

Before the Senior Classic race I wanted to do a quick lap of the track in my Opel Manta Berlinetta and drop off the guy who was signalling for me at the Bungalow. I hopped back in the car but was told by a guy when I got to Windy Corner that the road was closing to traffic. *'Shit, I was in danger of missing the race.'* So I drove past him, the sweat now starting to pour as I worried about not getting back in time for the start. I was heading down to the Creg ny Baa when I saw the policeman standing in the middle of the track diverting cars and bikes off the circuit. So I pulled up alongside him and explained I have to carry on as I'm in the race. He wasn't having any of it and insisted I leave the road. Panic set in.

"Listen, I'm fucking Rob McElnea, I'm in the race".

"I don't care. I don't give a monkey's who you think you are, get off the track"

Shit. I can't go with the rest of the traffic and get stuck on the tight, twisting country roads as I would definitely not make it back in time. Only one thing for it.

I reversed the car back, slipped into first gear then floored the accelerator and watched the copper jump over my bonnet. There was a huge crowd already gathered at the Creg to watch the race and they went mental, cheering as I shot down toward the start-finish line a few miles away. When I got there I hid the car around the back of the paddock and then ran over to the Suzuki awning all the while crapping myself. Were the police waiting for me? So far, so good. It looked like I'd got away with it. I changed into my leathers and was walking up to the grid when I was collared for a pre-race chat, broadcast over the circuit.

I thought this was a good time to apologise to the police for what I'd done so I said *sorry* then went and won the race. There were big celebrations at the hotel that night and I'd forgotten all about what happened at the Creg until coppers turned up at the party, threatening to take me away. It was flippin' scary for a while and I thought I was for the high jump but maybe they were just winding me up as in the end they wished me well for the rest of the week .

As for the win, I've seen the pictures and I was white as a ghost at the end. The bike was just brilliant. The GS XR69 1000 cc was just a beautiful machine, perfect for the TT. It was a bit torquey, a little heavy but it was so forgiving, everything just worked perfectly and what a feeling to get that chequered flag then cruise up victory lane. Totally amazing. The win meant I would definitely get a contract from Suzuki for the following year and I could carry on working making my way towards the Grand Prix arena.

From the moment I first signed for Suzuki in December or January, from that day, when you put your signature on the contract, you're thinking about the TT. So to then have that day, when it's all over, you've finished the race and you've won, following six months of build up, then for it all to finish and stop on such a high, well the emotions were incredible. If it had gone the other way and turned out shit then I don't know what it might have been like. As it was, the remaining six months of that season were brilliant. We were flying at home on the short circuits plus I had wildcard entries in the 500 GPs. So from that massive high at the TT I was feeling good. I was confident I could impress at Grand Prix level and the few rides that I had in the World championship went really well. So I was bouncing going into 1984 on the promise of having another decent year. I also knew the next TT would be my last. Whatever happened, whatever the outcome on the track, no-one knew about my decision apart from me. I'd arrived at the conclusion in January that whatever contracts they put in front of me this would be my last journey to race at the Isle of Man. I loved everything about it but I just didn't want to ride there anymore. I was getting faster on the short circuits where you could take a lot of risks. You could almost have the front wheel folding into every corner and that was the way I was sort of riding every weekend. At the TT I could take it back a little bit but I was still a fairly fast rider. I also felt the law of averages were against you the more you raced the Isle of Man.

It was a weird thing having this secret to myself. I hadn't even told my girlfriend or family. I was shitting myself all the way leading up to the TT and then crapping myself all the way through it. I don't really know how I managed to ride so well. Once you get on the track with every practice session, every lap, you just get into it, focus and forget about everything else. I was running well and because I was feeling sharp, I was loving it again but all the time it was like *'right, that's one race done. Two more races. Nuts, it's Friday, it's almost all over.'* It was a real edgy week.

It all started with the unbelievably shit-your-pants Formula One race when I was riding the 750. That was the scariest race I've ever ridden and that's because it wasn't a very good bike. It wasn't fast enough so you had to ride the wheels off it and rev it like mad. It had a 16-inch front wheel on it and was built for scratching around flipping Donington Park, it was not a road racing bike at all. In the race I was in the top three so realised I was doing all right. Then I went into Hillberry on the pitstop lap and as I flicked it into the right hand turn the steering damper exploded! I had a massive wobble and with the bike out of control, brushed the wall with my shoulder. I somehow made it back to the pits. I used to ride with quite a lot of steering damper so when I pulled in I told my mechanic what had happened. He replied

"Oh, just do one more lap and pull in".

I'm thinking *"are you having a laugh?"*

Literally every time you opened the throttle the front wheel went a fraction light. Every gear change and every time you got near the power it would just shake out of your hands. So I filled up with fuel, set off again and even as I headed down Bray Hill it was wobbling. So scary. I managed a few more miles until I was approaching the Crosby pub and as I hit the little rises the bike blew up! Thank God for that. I'm convinced had that not happened I would never have survived had I carried on. I should have just said I'm not going back out but in the heat of the middle of the race, in that brief half-a-minute or so and your Chief mechanic says *'carry on'*, well. So I was flippin' lucky about that. It was the first race of the week of my last ever week at the TT, which didn't start off too well. I just had the 500 Senior on the Wednesday plus the Classic on Friday to get through and then that was it.

In contrast the RG500 was brilliant. I'd just arrived at the TT, flying in from Germany having raced 500 Grand Prix at Salzburg and Nurburgring where I'd been on the front row. My team had set off behind me going across Europe by road. My mechanic Junior Collins and the UK team were there in the Island with my 1000 F1 bike so I started practising with that. Then the 500 team turned up on Monday so we got that ready. That meant I had a bit of practice on the 500 so come Wednesday I was back in love with racing. Properly loved it. It was that weird race where Joey forgot to stop for fuel. We were flying in beautiful conditions. As much as I loved the 500 it was hard work around there, a little bit buzzy and bouncy but brilliant fun. I was riding that bike at Grand Prix so hard it just became part of me. I could do anything with it and just felt totally on fire on it. During the race I was having pit signals saying 'plus this' and 'plus that' as I diced for the lead with Joey Dunlop and then all of a sudden I got a board that said something like 'minus 30'. So I thought *'fucking hell, if Joey's going that fast he can freakin' have it.'* I then came around the Black Hut/Mountain Box with my visor fogging, I'd used all of my tear-offs so I had trouble peering out from my helmet yet as I came through I could just make out this figure sat on the bank with a yellow helmet waving at me. *'You are joking. It's bloody Joey.'* I couldn't believe it. So with him out of the race I'm leading but all of a sudden the bike started to rattle. Or so I thought. Up until now all I'd heard was a bit of wind noise before I saw Joey's helmet and next thing, in my mind, I could hear the engine falling to bits while the flipping crankshaft was jumping out so I almost rode all the way home with the clutch in. The reality was there was nothing wrong and the bike was performing brilliantly. It was when I had time to think about the winners circle the imaginary rattles started.

Then we had the Classic on Friday which I won. So it had been an amazing week and then I literally had a private plane taking me to the UK then flying on to Paul Ricard in France. That's when I told everyone about my decision not to ride at the TT anymore. I said to Rex White at Suzuki *'it's been absolutely brilliant but that's it'*. It was also such a relief for my girlfriend when I told her that I didn't want to ride at the TT anymore. It wasn't that I had anything against the TT, I just wanted to do something else. It had been good to me and I loved every second of my time there but that was enough as far as I was concerned. So, that was it. You can imagine the feeling of winning those two races, having had this burden in my mind *'I've just gotta get through these few laps, I've just got to get through it safely'*. I'd carried that weight since the start of the year and then come Friday of race week it had all finished on a high. So the release of telling people that it's all over was absolutely insane. It was amazing it turned out the way it did with me on the top step of the podium. It was a team effort though and Junior Collins and the boys at Suzuki were brilliant with my bike preparation and making sure I had everything I needed.

We all knew how dangerous the TT could be yet in my short time there I never saw anything. You knew the bits that were scary and the parts you had to have so much respect for. Back then the circuit was really scary, it was so bumpy at places you could fall off just by the bike shaking and chattering. You could easily end up hitting the ground going through Quarry Bends just by being in the wrong spot of the surface. It was that bad. However, you knew all that, so you had a lot of respect for it. As soon as you close your visor, you don't attack it like you would Redgate at Donington Park; instead you're going kerb to kerb in fifth gear and it's all about keeping that throttle open. There are sections where it looks like it should be second gear yet you click in fifth and the road just opens in front of you. That final year I did quite a few pillion laps on Mad Sunday with some Suzuki head honchos. You could feel them on the back, nearly gripping you in half because they don't know what's coming. It would look like we should be back shifting, braking for the corner but you then click up one into fifth gear and you can feel them squeezing the life out of you. The road just opens up like that and these are the places where you have to be committed. Obviously I thought about the danger, my career, what I wanted to do and the consequences of things going wrong with the TT but when you're riding you just kept saying *'get on with it'*. You gotta ride it as if you love it and I did. I think that was why I went so well because from the first time I set off in that Manx Grand Prix I totally loved it which made it easier to learn, I wasn't forcing anything. In fact, I never forced anything anywhere, so it all came to me quite naturally. I rode the Manx and TT with such a buzz and therefore so much enjoyment

I was back at the TT in 1992 but this time as a team manager. That was running the Loctite Yamaha with Carl Fogarty and that was horrible. By then things had changed a lot. From the period when I raced there in the early 1980s to a decade later all the sports bikes had turned into more short circuit type weapons so they weren't ideal for the TT plus Foggy was such an animal when he was riding, you were totally crapping it. When I was the racer you were nervous but all your focus is on your bike, your setup and you hitting the spots around the course. When you go as a team manager you have to think of absolutely everything. You're just crapping it the whole fortnight. You keep checking *'is the bike bolted together properly, is it gonna do this, is it gonna do that'*. You're trying to make the bike as good as possible for them but I didn't enjoy the experience at all. I'd gone back to the TT the year before for the first time since quitting in '84 and was running Brian Morrison on the Loctite Yamaha. I'd raced for them in World Superbike and was still with them in 1991 albeit in the British championship so I was still fairly sharp. Brian wouldn't ride with a steering damper despite my best efforts to persuade him to do so. I always had the steering damper on so if the front wheel popped off the ground it landed straight yet Brian never turned it on. During practice he was complaining about this and that so I suggested he put more damper on but he hated it. I think he was one of those racers who liked to have more feel in the bike whereas I was always riding with the front wheel popping up all the time as I liked it landing straight. I had a chance to see for myself how it was handling as I had a guest ride in the parade lap. I set off on Brian's bike alongside Ron Haslam who was on the Norton and immediately I had a massive wobble going down Bray Hill. So I pulled in a mile or so further down the road at Braddan, adjusted the steering damper for what seemed like ages and then set off like a nutter.

Wow! It was totally brilliant blasting along because I remembered the track so crystal clear. If someone had said to me *'Rob, we'll close the roads, go put your suit on and have a blast on the TT course'* I'd have bitten their hand off and now here was my chance. It's in the middle of race day, the crowds are huge, there's loads of people watching, beautiful, sunny conditions so I wasn't wasting this opportunity. I just clicked into it and did something like a 112mph lap even with stopping plus I wanted to blast Ronnie as well. He was just doing what everyone in the parade lap should be doing and that was riding around waving to everybody. I thoroughly enjoyed it even if I did get a bollocking for riding like that. Looking back I can't remember what setting Brian eventually used but he took a third place in the F1 race and finished fourth in the Senior, which was okay.

As far as Carl Fogarty was concerned twelve months later, well, I tried to like him but back then he wasn't that likeable a guy really. We jumped through hoops trying to get the bike right for him. It was hard work, he was moaning but he was right because the bike wasn't right. We eventually got it better but the way he rode, I don't know how he did so well at the TT. You put his and Steve Hislop's styles together; they were totally chalk and cheese. Hizzy was so easy on the eye, so smooth and much more in terms of a thinking man in what you needed to do at the TT. This wasn't in Foggy's nature but on the flipside I guess it's why he ended up being a multiple world champion. All in all, I didn't enjoy my time as a TT team boss, it was pretty hard work.

I was back at the TT again in 2007 this time as part of the Centenary celebrations. I was going to ride Tommy Hill's British Superbike in the parade lap. It was a really crazy hot day. My Dad had flown in to watch Agostini and all of the other big names taking part. As I was being called out to the grid he started to feel unwell so I was concerned about his welfare and thinking of knocking it on the head but I think it was TAS racing boss Philip Neill who said he would be alright as he would take care of him. So I set off but my head wasn't in the right place. I gassed it away and made myself dizzy going from first to second gear and I don't think my brain ever caught up. I was wobbling around behind Phil Read who was on this annoyingly noisy thing doing about 50 miles an hour. I thought *'I can't stand this'* so I passed him on the run through to Glen Helen. Before the start John McGuinness had warned me there was oil down at Sarah's cottage and I'm going

"fuck's sake John, I'm not going fast, I don't need to worry about that."

Then I get to Sarah's cottage. Now if I was to sit with you and tell you a lap around the TT course I would be inch perfect but put me on a bike and try to do it at warp factor it doesn't work, it's all wrong. Everybody knows, you come out of Glen Helen in second gear then shut the throttle and just keep it shut for that right hander at Sarah's then keep it shut longer than normal because then it opens up on the climb onto the Cronk y Voddy straight. So you go second gear, keep the throttle closed and then closed, closed, closed, then the corner goes tight and you open up and go. This time I go second gear, third gear, then flick it and I'm going *'Oh my fucking God'*. As I've flicked it I don't know where I am so then I've just thrown it on its side. I've got everything on the floor, my knee, my elbow, it's all on the ground. I just go through the oil then ride straight into the bank. I didn't actually fall off and slide into the bank, I actually rode into it with my knee still on the ground. So that spat me off and the bike went up into a tree. it was horrendous. I was that close. It scarred me for a long time. I just wanted to get out of there as quickly as possible. I was soon on a flight with my Dad and flew away. No hanging around. It took me probably six months to get over. I was constantly thinking about everything I've ever done and yet I could easily have not come home from that. Nothing on the line, no race to win, no title at stake, no job to earn or hold onto. Just a parade lap. I had the wife and kids at home and I was thinking all sorts of Mike Hailwood stories and what happened to him, things like that. It took me ages to get over it. I laughed along with everybody else whenever it was mentioned but inside I was really shaken up.

From then on I never wanted to get on a race bike again. I just wasn't getting the buzz that I used to. I had the likes of Niall MacKenzie and James Whitham insisting I have a blast at a track day but it just didn't appeal any more. I was a stone and a half heavier than in my racing days so getting on a motorcycle was hard work plus I was more happier on a trials bike which is my real passion. After what I had done in my career, I couldn't do it anymore. I was simply no longer interested. I did actually go back in 2014 for a parade lap in the Classic TT as part of the Joey's Rivals celebrations but even now, I don't remember too much about it.

Rob's impact on the Isle of Man was much bigger than the one he made at Sarah's Cottage on his centenary visit with a results record comparable with the likes of World Champion Giacomo Agostini who he would go on to ride for in the 500cc GP Marlboro Yamaha team alongside Eddie Lawson. He would also partner Kevin Schwantz at Pepsi Suzuki before a brief stint in World Superbike. Rob was crowned British 750 champion and then went onto run a highly successful British Superbike team as well as the Virgin one-make Yamaha championships.

Having retired from racing he now divides his time between Scunthorpe and Gran Canaria with his wife and their two children.

STEVE PLATER

Born Luton, England

TT Years 2007-09
14 races, 2 wins, 1 x 2nd, 3 x 4th, 1 x 5th, 1 x 7th, 2 x 8th, 2 x 10th, 1 x 15th, 1 x DNF

Steve Plater enjoyed a short but very successful TT career making his debut during the Centenary celebrations of 2007. He was 34 by this time and became one of very few riders to score a Mountain course victory in only his second year at the Isle of Man. He followed that by adding his name to a prestigious list of Senior race winners in what would be his last TT outing. He also set sector records one of which, from Bungalow to Cronk ny Mona, would last for an incredible 9 years eventually being broken by Peter Hickman when he recorded the first ever 135mph lap.

I had no interest in the Isle of Man TT races as a youngster but then again the same could be said of motorcycle road racing in general. My passion as a kid was Grasstrack and then Speedway. I'd never even heard of the TT. That's not me being smart, it just wasn't on my radar. I thought Grand Prix racing was for those who didn't know how to go sideways on a motorbike. That was kind of my outlook. I had a dabble at Speedway when I was 15 but financially I couldn't afford it and neither could my Dad. I did the usual things that a teenager does including an apprenticeship laying bricks. I tried other bits and bobs like stockcars and banger racing, that kind of thing, which I think is far more crazy than riding the TT course. Forty to fifty idiots trying to kill each other in an oval stadium and there's no getting out. You could say that was my upbringing.

My road riding started off with a Phantom 175 that my Dad had bought for 40 quid. I couldn't wait to get my hands on a moped so there I was, at six o'clock in the morning on my 16th birthday, sitting on it with a grin on my face; I lasted three days before I was in hospital.

I ditched the moped for proper road bikes and in 1993 went to Cadwell Park with a few mates. I signed a piece of paper, handed over £110 and for that I had around 20 laps on a Honda VFR 400 with all the kit supplied. The instructors were all top class racers and they were saying to me '*You're really good, you should go racing*.'

I thought they were only saying that to get me to come back and spend some more money.

I did another track day at the end of the year and at the safety briefing there were two young lads, both on brand new Yamaha YZF 750s spouting off about how they were going to do this and going to do that and I'm stood there wide eyed thinking '*Bloody hell, is this what happens on a flippin' track day?*' By the end of the day I'd smoked them both and it was then that I thought to myself, '*Do you know what? I need to sell this bike and get something to go racing on*.' I had been riding around on the roads with my mates like a psychopath at over 150 miles an hour and somehow getting away with it. I finally realised if I carried on like that it would end in tears. That's how my career kicked off.

March 13th, 1994 is a date I will never forget as it was the day of my first ever race. I'd sold my GSXR and got myself a four year old Honda CBR 600 purely because that was the biggest bike I was allowed to ride as a newcomer wearing an orange vest and I went and won on it in my very first outing. It was in an Open race at Cadwell Park and I was up against a lot of big bikes; for me it was like winning a MotoGP.

My career progressed and in 1995 I made my road racing debut at the NorthWest 200 and marked it by crashing my year old purple CBR

600 going into Juniper chicane; just a case of me going in too hot on the brakes, onto the grass and down I went. That was a steep learning curve. I'd been to the NorthWest as a spectator two years earlier when Carl Fogarty did the double and I was hooked, not just with the racing but the social side as much as anything. That's how my road racing career started off. By now, I was fully aware of the TT but it was just something that everybody else did; it wasn't a road I'd thought of riding.

In 1996 I moved up to the British Supercup which was the forerunner of BSB and managed to do a few rounds plus there was the Shell Oils British championship, which I managed to win and two years later I was racing for the Sanyo Honda team in the British championship. They were run by expert tuner Russell Savory with ex-racer Mick Grant as team manager. He, of course, was a TT race winner and it could well have been through him that I spoke with the organisers and agreed to race at the TT despite not being offered any financial incentive to do so. As I wasn't going to be paid I said I'd only ride on the condition they wouldn't use my name in terms of PR or promotion. Ahead of the TT I went to the Island with a few mates on something of a jolly, did a few laps, purely to see what it was all about. I liked what I saw and was up for it but as the event drew closer I suddenly had all manner of bike journalists on the phone asking me about my upcoming involvement with the TT. I enquired as to who had put them up to this to be told it was the organisers. So I was on the phone to the Isle of Man and told them they'd broken the deal therefore I wasn't going. Honda had already sent the bikes to the Isle of Man by this point so I spoke with them, explained the situation as to why I wasn't doing it and they backed me. So that was that and the bikes were used as spares at that year's event. I didn't hold a grudge against the TT. I just thought they should have been paying me to go. Looking back I'm pleased I didn't race there because it was probably a bit too early for me. I was very loose back then and not scared of anything which is the wrong mentality.

I then spent many years in British Superbike and World Endurance as well as the NorthWest of course when the thought of racing at the TT

"I had Mick Grant in my ear, breaking it all down into sections and learning it that way because you can't even explain a corner at the TT until you've ridden around it."

STEVE PLATER

cropped up again. I pondered about going in 2006 but thought if I did I may come under the spotlight given how well I was doing at other road race events so therefore decided to wait a year which of course would be the Centenary TT and with every man on the grid wanting to win then maybe I could slip in somewhat unnoticed. There was a new organising team in place following my previous attempt to take part and they were much more open to dealing with me, financially as well. We had a big discussion where I stated I wanted to be competitive and if, at the end of practice I wasn't happy, I would go home and they could have their money back. You don't know if once you get to the TT you're going to like it. It's unlike any other race on the planet.

From the moment I said yes the plan was to get over to the island and do as much homework as I possibly could. I had Mick Grant in my ear, breaking it all down into sections and learning it that way because you can't even explain a corner at the TT until you've ridden around it. I didn't do exactly what he said because everybody's different but it was fabulous to have a TT winner and very successful Grand Prix rider giving you the correct mindset on how to go about doing it.

I'm one of those that can't fathom too much out from watching an onboard camera because it's not the same view as your own vision when you're buzzing around so I spent most of my time learning the circuit in a hire car even though I was offered motorcycles to use. As there is so much to take in I found that easier than being on a bike where you're also concentrating to keep yourself safe.

On one occasion I was in a car with my then girlfriend and now wife Vicky as a passenger taking notes. We were due to fly home but I thought we could squeeze a lap in before heading to the airport. Some parts of the course have no speed limit so at times we were flying around, bearing in mind we had a flight to catch. We were motoring down from the top of Barregarrow, flat out, coming to the notorious bottom part yet unbeknown to me temporary traffic lights had been set up as part of some roadworks. As we turned the corner there they were, the light was on red but there was no way we would stop in time so I had to commit and go through. Next thing, I'm clipping cones and things are flying in the air. Thankfully nothing was coming the other way as the cars on the other side hadn't set off. We got through okay, the pair of us stunned into silence for what seemed like an awful long time. It was one of those moments. Vicky still reminds me of that to this day especially if she's questioning my driving.

Fellow competitors never really tell you what they think of you as a racer even if they thought you're mental or too aggressive on a bike, nobody actually tells you to your face. When some folk heard I was doing the TT there were a lot saying *'that idiot's gonna end up in a box before he comes back'* plus *'he shouldn't be going'*. No one ever said it to my face but there were plenty of comments on social media even back then. I knew my parents were uneasy about it as too was my wife but I knew they would never stand in my way.

My first time down Bray Hill on closed roads on a bike was behind the travelling marshal and believe me, that's the best way to do it as a newcomer. It just breaks the ice, you know you're not on your own, which helps enormously. We're still averaging over a hundred miles an hour and it doesn't help when Keith Amor, who was also making his debut, is buzzing around as if we're racing. I was laughing to myself *"give me a bit of space"* but he was getting on my nerves more than anything else. Riding behind the marshall was the perfect way to break yourself into the course because there's a lot of things you can't fathom out until you've actually ridden around. On my first time on my own through Union Mills in practice I knew I wouldn't be going home. The only scary thing I found was the concentration side. I didn't have any moments yet if you look at footage of me at Barregarrow you can hear the crowd screaming when I go through and around the bend at the bottom. Even John McGuinness had a word with me saying *'what are you doing?'* On each lap I was taking what I thought was the racing line as it was fast but perhaps a bit too near the knuckle. I learnt another valuable lesson coming out of Parliament Square, accelerating up to the right hander at May Hill when, suddenly, on the right hand side of the road, somebody stuck a pit board out for me. I'm like *'is that for me?'* so I read it, looked forward again and was already going far too fast into May Hill. I nearly hit the kerb on the left hand side which, if I had, would have had me going through the hedge. It was a massive, massive lesson. I still don't know to this day who gave me the pit board. It taught me very quickly to completely ignore everything unless it was a flag. From that moment every time I was circulating around the course I wouldn't respond to fans or anything else for that matter because you just cannot afford to be distracted in the slightest. However, I had enjoyed qualifying and not gone home. My mindset for year one was, we'll get to the end of the TT and then make a decision towards the end of the season, as to whether I'll go back.

Even though there was plenty going on around the Island being the Centenary TT, it kind of passed me by as I was so focused on learning the course, that's all that mattered. My wife was there with me with our newborn daughter. The TT was changing fast and becoming a great worldwide event again having been somewhat through the doldrums so it was good to be involved as a competitor. I was happy with everything, I didn't make any setup changes, I kept saying to the boys, just leave it, as I was getting faster every lap and if things aren't right then I'll shut off the throttle. That's what we did.

I can't express how happy I was with a tenth place finish in the Superbike TT, my first race especially with such a strong field with the likes of John McGuinness, Bruce Anstey, Cameron Donald and Guy Martin to name a few. So I had a good debut year. My quickest lap was 125.3mph which made me the fastest ever newcomer and that wasn't beaten until Josh Brookes arrived in 2013. I wanted to return to the TT the following year but held back on making a decision because I needed to make sure I was doing the right thing. Come autumn I made the commitment and set myself a three year plan to try to be as competitive as possible as well as give me the time to win a TT.

So I was back in the Isle of Man for TT 2008 with a rocket ship of a Yamaha R6. It was the same bike I used in the British championship and thanks to the engine genius that was Steve Mellor it had obliterated everyone at the NorthWest, it felt like the fastest thing on the planet. It was embarrassingly quick. I knew after year one, I was really fast over the Mountain. Anything that's quick seems to suit me better than slower sections, even on short circuits. The first Supersport clash of the week was going like a dream. I was running in third place in the race, which for me was incredible, I would be on the podium in only my second year. Over the Mountain on the last lap I made up five seconds over McGuinness to move into second place which I couldn't believe as he was the King of the Mountain. I was made up to stand on the rostrum in the runner-up spot behind Bruce Anstey. However, as soon as we walked down from the podium there was talk of a problem with Bruce's bike which was being stripped in the scrutineering bay. I've always said publicly that on that day, Bruce would have won the race on a bog standard road bike straight out of the showroom, because that's how good he is. However, someone in the team had effectively fitted a sidecar engine which, for me, was an insult to his ability. That person, whether they were aware or not, wasn't just cheating me in second or John in third, it was unfair on every man on that grid all the way down the order. So Bruce had the win he deserved taken away from him with the victory going to me because of someone else's misdoings. It's a bloody shame for any race to be decided like that plus I never got to spray the podium in first place, however it is on record as my TT win and I'm very, very proud of it.

My biggest problem at the TT was that I would always seem to start the race too slowly. It's not natural to get out of bed, wander about for four or five hours, then throw a leg over a bike and immediately be on record pace. So that was a weakness as far as I was concerned. Also at the TT everything's got to be right. You've only got to look at Bruce Anstey who will just pull out of a race if he's not feeling right. It doesn't have to be the bike, if everything is not clicking then what's the point in just circulating. It's a dangerous arena, so I fully understand when someone pulls in and says *'that's enough'*.

In terms of the Superbike that year the Yamaha wasn't the greatest handling wise. I was still inexperienced in terms of setting up the R1 at the TT. It was quite new and we'd come from BSB which of course is a totally different racing environment. We had new TTX shocks which were too close to the exhaust and therefore not working properly as they were overheating. The hardest part was making it rideable. John McGuinness followed me along the Cronk y Voddy straight and said he was more scared by what my Yamaha was doing than I was. I'm still learning at that time and would roll off the throttle if it was an issue so I wasn't too worried. Yet the big bikes is where it's at at the TT, they are the races everybody wants to win, especially the Senior at the end of the week

Soon after the TT wound up that year I had a call from Neil Tuxworth who wanted me to race the HM Plant Honda for them in 2009 which meant the NorthWest 200, the TT plus the British Supersport championship. This was what I'd be aiming for. I'd practically gone full circle from where I was in 2003 on a factory Honda. I had a busy build up to TT09 eventually flying into the Island from Thruxton in a private plane to get there on time. I'd had plenty of experience on my 600 which I'd been riding in British Supersport most weekends plus I'd also had some outings on the Superbike in BSB so I arrived at the TT very much at ease with things. Practice went well, I now had John McGuinness as a teammate, he was still very much the man to beat around there. However, unbeknown to me, he was feeling the pressure of me being in the team. I was number one at the NorthWest at the time and he was the top dog at the TT. I think that's why Neil Tuxworth brought me in to keep John on his toes, not that I think he needed it because he would still do everything he could to win even if he was on his own.

Practice that year went well, the weather was generally good and I would have a good start to race week. Again, I was slow off the line in the Superbike TT. I wasn't really on the pace at the beginning plus I didn't really expect to challenge John. I was probably closer to him in that first race than I thought I would be and finishing in second place to make it a Honda one-two was something special with the extra bonus of standing on a TT podium with two legends in Valentino Rossi and Giacamo Agostini, who were there to hand out the prizes.

Senior race day was long. We'd had the Supersport and Superstock races earlier in the week but now it was the climax, the big one. I'd been my usual self throughout that TT, playing catch up each time after the first half of lap one in each race. Neil Tuxworth had mentioned this to me, somewhat in jest but on the other hand in all seriousness because he is there to iron out any weaknesses you may have, to try and get the best from you. I was away at number seven in the Senior and with no-one at number six there was a bit of a gap on the road ahead. In the early part of the race and especially as Guy Martin started ten seconds behind me, I managed to up my game early on and stayed close enough to John to put him under pressure. Deep down I didn't expect to beat him plus we were both lucky because the man that had been on the pace during practice was injured and that was Cameron Donald. If he'd been fit and replicating that speed then he would have been involved at the front. This time I'd definitely got my ass in gear much earlier than usual having treated it a bit like a mass start short circuit race. John opened up a lead, a handy one but not too comfortable, while I was in second place. I came in for my second pit stop and the boys told me that John was out of the race.

"*Fucking hell, is he okay?*"

"*Yeah, don't worry. He's fine*"

"*Okay*" I replied and set off again down pit lane but this time as race leader

It was the longest, longest two laps of my life. Unbelievably long, especially the last one. The only thing that could have beaten me was mechanical failure. I didn't know what happened to John, in fact his chain had snapped at Ramsey but what I did know, if there was a concern with the bike then they would have retired me there and then. As it was they said nothing so I got my head down and cracked on. I will never forget racing across the Mountain then coming out of the Creg with all the people sitting with their legs hanging over the bank, waving and going berserk. I had to ignore them, trying to stay focused because I didn't want to lose concentration and make the stupidest mistake, perhaps at Governor's Dip. There was no time for wheelies or any other kind of celebrations until I saw the chequered flag in the distance. I'd only ridden something like a dozen TT races so I couldn't risk anything going wrong. Then across the line and what a feeling, like you just cannot describe.

Things may have been different had John's chain not snapped or Cameron had not hurt himself when he crashed during practice on the approach to Keppel Gate. He would have been on the pipe for sure if that hadn't happened. He could even have beaten John, he was riding that well. It's easy to forget where Cameron was at that point of his career because he was never as good again. If he hadn't tipped off on that left then the TT could have been a whole different place for the next couple of years.

My Dad was doing my pit board at Hailwood Heights, he'd just given me my P1 and wanted to get back to the pits for the presentation. The only way to get back from there was to get the electric tram from the Bungalow down to Laxey then along the coast road to Douglas. However there was a massive queue. Undeterred he just went straight to the front of the line which I suppose you can do if, like him, you're a big, burly twenty-stone man who used to run the doors in Luton when we lived there. In all fairness he was also carrying the pitboard with my name on so everyone in the queue was peaking anyway and treating him like royalty. He managed to get back for the celebrations too which was wonderful.

From crossing the line onwards there is so much happening that it's too much to take in. John McGuinness mentions it a lot. It feels like a massive weight being lifted off your shoulders after the Senior. You're not really taking much notice as the thought the TT is over and you've made it through the week is very much on your mind and that relief is enormous. You're obviously emotional when you're on the run back down the pit lane which is fabulous and turn into the winner's enclosure to see the team and how emotionally happy they are, from your mechanics, your visor changer, tyre people, everyone. It's all busy with TV interviews and all the other media then the podium which isn't that big a part because there's so much going on. I don't mean that disrespectfully, it's a bloody good happy memory but there's lots happening. There's the post-race press conference followed by the chit chats in the hospitality unit which is a bit like they do in BSB. Probably the most powerful memory I have, of which I'm so happy and proud of, was Murray Walker coming over and talking to me. He knew everything about my career and I was just knocked out by him. We spent some time chatting which was absolutely bloody brilliant because he's such a legend and it meant more to me than being with Ago and Rossi on the podium for the first race. The TT fans are brilliant so I always try to make time for them, plus, being the last race of the week the trophy presentation was on the stage behind the Grandstand in front of everybody. So there was lots to do, I still hadn't had a shower at this point and all I wanted to do was get cleaned up and be on my own.

The next thing I knew it was six o'clock at night. Everybody's packing the trucks up preparing to leave the Island. What I was looking forward to was meeting my Dad for a pint at the Queen's Hotel on Douglas promenade. I left Vicky and the baby in the motorhome and walked down from the paddock towards the Castle Mona hotel. As I got to the steep hill at the Arches on Mona Drive I started reflecting on what had happened that day. Within moments I was bawling my eyes out as all my emotions kicked in as l realised what I'd done. I had to sit down on a bench halfway down the hill as I was still taking it all in. I spent a few minutes looking up at the sky thinking about everything, getting myself back together. I was wondering *'where do i go from here?'* I didn't start racing until I was 26 so I knew I was always going to struggle to do anything in terms of World Championship racing. As I was such a late starter racing I was always kind of in a rush to win things. As it was I had no intention of going back and trying to win as many TTs as I could.

I was also British Supersport champion in 2009 but if that was a great year then 2010 wasn't. I was still with Honda but racing in Superstock and had the perfect start to the season, winning the first few races with a lap record at every track so I was comfortably leading the championship when I went to the NorthWest. However my season effectively ended there and then when the front folded as I went into Quarry Hill at around 125 mph and I crashed and broke my arm.

The following year I signed for Padgett's to do British Supersport plus I agreed to ride for the Honda TT Legends team in the World Endurance championship. However, a big crash at Thruxton just before the TT saw me break my arm again causing a lot of nerve damage in the process. That didn't finish my career, I came back and was still getting on the podium but my concern was damaging myself further. I knew I was no spring chicken. I wasn't going to get a Superbike ride. So it was time to knock it on the head but without confirming my retirement.

Suddenly I found myself busy with other things plus I was offered a TV commentary role at the TT in 2011 so that Thruxton crash could be viewed as having something of a silver lining. All-in-all I felt I couldn't achieve what I wanted to so there's no real point in carrying on to a certain degree. I didn't really feel like I had to announce a retirement anyway because it's my business and hey, you never know what could be around the corner.

Steve is probably busier now than when he was a full-time racer. Living in Woodhall Spa with wife Victoria and their two daughters at the time of writing he's Team Manager for the BMW Synetiq Motorrad team in the British Superbike championship. He's also test ridden for Norton plus tyre manufacturers and is the rider liaison officer at the North West 200. He's also in demand for media work most notably as one of the presenters for the TV coverage of the Isle of Man TT and Manx Grand Prix races plus hosts chat shows involving competitors of all forms of motorsport.

BRIAN REID

Born Dromore, Northern Ireland

TT Years 1981-1994
45 races, 5 x wins, 3 x 2nd, 2 x 3rd, 3 x 4th, 1 x 5th, 1 x 9th, 1 x 10th, 1 x 18th, 1 x 19th, 1 x 20th, 2 x 21st, 24 x DNF

MGP 1978-80
1 x 2nd, 3 x DNF

Brian Reid is undoubtedly one of the finest riders to come out of Northern Ireland. He boasts not only five TT triumphs but also two Formula Two TT World championship titles in a racing career spanning almost two decades. Had he not been plagued with unreliable machinery then surely his trophy tally would have been greater. A two-stroke specialist he proved equally adaptable and successful on bigger and more powerful motorbikes. He's also one of an exclusive band of riders to win two TT races in a week

I've known motorcycle racing all my life. My uncle Ian McGregor was Irish champion in the 60s and 70s and when I was a kid, I used to go to the races with him, all the way through his career until he retired in 1976 which was the year I started. It was through him that I developed my interest and it became all I ever wanted to do. As a kid I'd buy all the books and magazines to read about all the great riders of that era. I grew up watching the likes of Mike Hailwood and Giacomo Agostini racing at the Ulster Grand Prix and had their names in my autograph book along with Phil Read, Bill Ivy, Jim Redman, Kel Carruthers, everybody, they're all in it. I still have the book. I also kept scrapbooks, mainly pictures of my uncle but all the TT heroes were in there. I'd look at the pictures and imagine what it must be like to race at the Isle of Man, especially going over Ballaugh Bridge. I'd seen hundreds of photographs of this iconic landmark and dreamt about what it must be like to ride over yet when I raced there for the first time it wasn't how I'd imagined at all: it was totally different to what I was expecting.

The very first time I went to the Isle of Man was in 1975 to watch the Manx Grand Prix. We were there to support Randall Cowell, a Manxman who sponsored my uncle, in fact he was riding Ian's bike that week. Randall had begun racing in 1960 so had been around a while. We stayed at his house and he'd often drive us around the circuit so I got a real feel for the place. I had to come back home for work, I was an apprentice engineer doing fabrication welding so I was only there for practice week but I enjoyed every moment.

The first bike I ever owned was a Triumph Tiger Cub that I bought for ten pounds. I was about nine years old and rode it around in nearby fields having taken off all the lights and the mudguard. A couple of years later my father bought a 250cc Greeves Silverstone motocross bike and I was soon flying about on that. There was no such thing as schoolboy motocross in Northern Ireland back then so it was a case of just mucking about. The first road racing bike I owned was a 250 TD3 Yamaha. I was eighteen at the time and I ploughed all my savings into that. I raced that for about eighteen months going along with my uncle Ian who was still competing at the time. There was no such thing as doing either short circuits or roads, everybody did both. So we entered all the Irish meetings. He also won at the Jurby road races in the Isle of Man which are no longer going.

I couldn't wait to race on the Mountain course and as soon as I had the money to get a new bike I did. My father lent me half of what I needed and I became the owner of a TZ 250 Yamaha. My uncle Ian encouraged me to get to the Isle of Man as soon as possible so in 1978 I put in my entry and set off on my own to the Manx Grand Prix. I didn't even have a van, all I had was the bike on a trailer, nothing to even tow it. There were a few lads going to the Manx from Northern Ireland so I got a lift in their van going across on the ferry and when we arrived in Douglas they dropped me off at Randall Cowell's house as I was using his garage. However, I was stuck as I had no transport; no car, no van, no nothing. I was fortunate to borrow a motorbike from the place where I was staying so I could travel back and forth to the garage. When practice came around I was stuck so I would put on the leathers and ride the race bike up to the paddock which was a couple of miles away. Every session I would do two laps and then retire at Braddan Bridge so I could get back to the garage from there as it was close by. Could you imagine anyone having to do that today? Up in the paddock I had no tools so the bike had to be ready to go when I left the house. I was on my own. Completely on my own. I had a room at the Seacliff guest house which was on Douglas promenade and there was a lad staying there with his wife who was from Northern Ireland. He'd hired a Mini for their holiday so he offered to run me around, help transport petrol and do other bits and pieces. I'd have been seriously stuck without his help, I was so fortunate to meet them. I still had to ride the bike to the paddock and was constantly dreading breaking down somewhere with no way of getting back. That was my life for two weeks. I was at the Seacliff as the owners, Ken and June Carson, who were originally from Northern Ireland, sponsored me for the two weeks by letting me stay there. We became real friends and I would always stay there in later years until they sold it and bought the Merridale Guest House which was just off the promenade by the Ascot Hotel so we followed them there too.

The Manx Grand Prix in 1978 was the first time they'd run a Newcomers race. I felt I had a chance of winning. Back home there were three groups of racing, A, B and C and I'd been doing well, quickly moving up to the top category. Having the new bike made a big difference so I arrived in the Island feeling confident. However there was another newcomer, a guy called Phil Mellor, who I'd never heard of. Every night when I looked at the practice times it was either him or me who was fastest; somehow during the week our paths never crossed. That kind of changed in the race as back then riders set off in pairs and our numbers were next to each other so we were together on the road although not for long. The weather conditions were atrocious and the bike seized at May Hill, throwing me off straight up the road and I ended up rolling along the footpath.That was the end of my Manx Grand Prix that year as the forks were bent amongst other things so I couldn't take part in the Junior race as planned. It wasn't the best meeting to make your Mountain course debut as generally weather conditions were poor for most of the fortnight, I didn't get enough laps and most sessions were either wet or foggy. It was a difficult few days. I thought I'd prepared well doing plenty of laps on open roads, just driving around and around plus I put in a fair bit of homework about the circuit but soon as I set off down Bray Hill i just felt lost again because you're going so much quicker so I had to almost relearn it again this time at racing speed. I had high hopes I could win it so I was disappointed that it didn't work out. Despite everything I loved my time there, the weather conditions and the crash didn't put me off. I just wanted to go back and do better.

As I was pouring my money into my racing I had none spare to go as a spectator to the TT in 1978 or '79. What a buzz that would have been to watch Mike Hailwood going around the circuit and I still regret not being able to afford it. I had to stay at home and listen to the radio, imagining what it would have been like to be there.

I was better organised when I returned to the Manx in 1979 with a bit more support from sponsors who'd bought a bike for me to ride plus I borrowed a van to get around easier than I had done on my debut. I now had a TZ 250F however my results weren't any better as the bike broke down. Even though it wasn't my bike I still had to pay for everything else which was a struggle. The exhaust on it cracked and I couldn't afford to buy a new one so it had to be welded; my big worry was that it would fall apart. It really was an achievement in those days to finish a Manx or a TT on a two-stroke. As it was, the Manx was pretty unremarkable for me in '79, I failed to finish the Junior race and to be honest, I don't actually remember much about that year at all.

The Junior race in 1979 was won by Clive Watts on a Suzuki RG500 and the following year he called to ask if I'd like to ride it at that year's Manx Grand Prix. At that stage I hadn't ridden anything bigger than a 250. I had a 350 for which I ended up borrowing an engine. I now had two bigger bikes, both of which I'd never ridden before. The Suzuki belonged to Ray Cowles and he completely refurbished the motor so it hadn't done anything in almost twelve months. On the first night of practice I set off but before I went he said to take it easy as everything in it was new and to wait until I was halfway round before giving it a blast. I nursed it to the 13th milestone when suddenly the big end seized. I was instantly worried that Ray would think I hadn't listened to him and had rode it flat out from the start. We got the bike back but missed valuable practice time as they had to split it and fit a new big end. As soon as it was fixed I took it out but the same thing happened again. I didn't manage a proper lap on it until Friday night and even then it was just one. We found out it was a bad batch of big ends that was causing the problem. So we went back to the old crankshafts that Clive had won on the year before and took it up to Jurby to run in new tyres and chain amongst other things in preparation for the race. Everything was running well and it seemed things were finally going our way until we went to put the bike into the back of the van. We were pushing it backwards when suddenly there was a loud '*clunk*' and the bike jammed in gear. What a nightmare that was! Ray rang Suzuki only to be told they couldn't get the parts to the airport to be flown over so we hired a taxi to collect them. As soon as they arrived Ray worked all through the night, stripping and fitting gearbox parts. The next day I was riding it down Bray Hill for the first time and feeling quite worried having not had much practice on it. It also had a nine gallon tank, which I could hardly see over. I was told not to worry about it and by the time I get to Ballacraine the weight will have dropped down. The bike was heavy to begin with and at one point I was leading but I eventually finished second behind race winner Geoff Johnson. For me, after all the hassle we'd had, it was an achievement just to make it to the finish.

I wanted to go to the Manx Grand Prix again in 1981 but I had new sponsors who insisted I compete at the TT. In a way it was against my wishes but by now I was winning races at home in Northern Ireland. Mick Mooney of Irish Racing Motorcycles bought a 350 for me while Alec Waugh supplied a 250 and that year I won my first Irish championship.

I was never one for pushing hard on a bike until I knew exactly where I was going and what I was doing. It took me a long time to feel comfortable on the TT circuit because of that. I wanted to ride smoothly and do things properly, not try and rush to get results. That was my mindset. I'd seen people go to the Isle of Man, approach it in a rough manner and somehow get away with it. I didn't want to do that. I wanted to try to survive. At first my parents didn't want me to race but I needed them to sign my licence when I started so they very reluctantly did so. I think once they saw how committed I was they were fully behind me and gave their support. Both of them were brilliant. By now I had my own business, doing engineering work by myself from home but it was getting to the stage where I was doing less because I was spending more time racing. Eventually it fizzled out completely once my motorcycling career took off.

The set-up at the TT didn't seem too different to the Manx. It was more professional and the competition was harder but apart from that it had the same feel. You knew you wouldn't win straight away so the aim really was to get to the finish and learn as much as you can along the way. I really hadn't done enough laps at the Manx due to weather and bike failures so my aim at that point was to gain more experience on the TT circuit.

I must confess I don't remember a lot about my first few years at the TT. In '81 I retired in the Junior 250 but got a bronze replica for coming nineteenth in the Senior. Twelve months later I won my first silver replica when I finished fourth in the 250. I do remember catching Paul Cranston in that race on the last lap but he was proving difficult to get past. I went by him and then he overtook me. I was becoming frustrated as it was unsettling my rhythm so in the end I stayed behind him across the finish line. I also had a TZ500 that year and picked up another bronze on that when I finished ninth in the Senior. That was a good year back home too as I became the first person to win three Irish championships in the same season, lifting the 250, 350 and 500 titles.

If I'd taken two steps forward in those couple of years then 1983 was definitely a step back. I'd planned to do some European rounds so I took on a guy to come to work for me. He'd spent time in Grand Prix plus he'd done a lot on sidecars and was highly recommended. Unfortunately he was a total disaster and everything just went wrong. At the TT I failed to finish a single race and by the time I went home I wasn't happy. I'd been fastest in practice on the 250 in the Junior so I had it in my head that I could win that. That ended when the bike seized going into Quarterbridge. It just wasn't working out with this mechanic. It was a nightmare, a terrible fortnight. Things came to a head when we were due to go to a race meeting one morning but the truck, with all the bikes in, wasn't there. Eventually it was found but in a smashed up state. Apparently, he'd got drunk, driven it and then crashed, writing it off in the process. All the bikes and gear were in a mess in the back. It was heartbreaking. Meanwhile, he cleared off and we never saw him again which was a blessing really as I was now tinkering for myself and from that point every race I entered I won..

Things could only get better at the TT the following year and thankfully, they did. Once more I had a 250 and 350 plus the RG 500 for the Senior. I still had a lot to learn at the TT but I was getting there. This time I was riding the EMC bike in the Junior, it was a good British machine and was going well in the race until on Glencrutchery Road, having just left the pits, it went down to one cylinder when the plug lead jumped off. I put it back on and set off but it came off again on the last lap so I stopped at Bishopscourt, stuck it back on and rode on for what became a very unsettling twenty miles or so. Thankfully, I had no further problems and crossed the finish line to score my first ever TT podium placing with Graeme McGregor, also on an EMC, taking the win ahead of Charlie Williams.

I'm never really thought of as a big bike rider but then again I was never really given a chance on a proper one. In the Senior TT that year I finished fourth behind race winner Rob McElnea with Roger Marshall and Trevor Nation completing the rostrum, all big guys with good reputations so perhaps I proved I could ride with the best no matter what machinery I was on. Losing all of my tear-offs didn't help my cause that day especially as there were so many flies around. I had to keep the visor open because you could barely see through it and I still don't know how I managed to finish that last lap.

There was not just the Isle of Man or Irish championships to contend with as I was drawn towards competing in the TT Formula 2 World championship. It was actually Mick Mooney's idea to build a F2 bike to race in the series so we ordered an engine but it didn't arrive until halfway through practice week at the TT. The situation worsened when we discovered we couldn't bolt it into our TZ frame because all the mountings were different. We managed to fit it eventually but it was a bit of a bodge job and once we got it out there in practice it went well enough, it seemed okay. Unfortunately, it didn't finish the race but it wasn't too far off the pace at the time it expired.

We went to Vila Real in Portugal for another meeting of the TT F2 championship where I finished on the podium. It was a hairy track which was more like a street circuit, based on the outskirts but went through part of the town. The extreme heat didn't help matters and a lot of people were collapsing, Joey Dunlop being one of them while Tony Rutter was even worse and had to have a drip attached due to a combination of heat exhaustion and dehydration. The next round was the Ulster Grand Prix. Everything was going well at Dundrod, I was leading by a country mile until the head stud broke and the bike packed in forcing me to retire. The final round was at Brno in Czechoslovakia and at that point I knew we couldn't win the championship but Mick Mooney insisted we went as he would have the engine ready. So I rode there and won which earned me a bronze medal for finishing third overall.

The following year, we built a completely new bike with an aluminium frame. This time we had a much better idea of what we were doing and enjoyed a lot of success. The final round of the TT F2 World championship was at my home circuit of Dundrod. I'd won in Portugal and Spain so had a chance of winning the title plus being the Ulster Grand Prix it made the occasion very special. However, I was feeling the pressure in front of the home crowd so it probably would have been better had the series ended somewhere else as you had journalists and other members of the media chasing after me when all I wanted was to be left alone to focus on what needed to be done. In the end I won the race and the World championship, which was an incredible feeling. That didn't last long though as I crashed in the very next race, breaking my femur which cut short any world title celebrations as I left Dundrod in an ambulance and spent the night in a hospital bed having had my leg pinned.

Things hadn't gone so well at the TT a few weeks earlier. I was leading the F2 race when the ignition packed up but that wasn't the end of it, there was more misfortune to come in the Junior. I started at number one and never saw anybody else really with mainly clear open roads ahead of me. The race was drawing to a close, I was leading by 12 seconds and in my head I'm thinking

"I've got it, I've got it, my first TT win, oh my God, I just hope Joey is still going so I can beat him fair and square."

As I came down from the Creg the bike started spluttering. I couldn't believe it. I was out of fuel. I toured in from Brandish and pulled over at Hillberry. A few seconds later Joey came by. I was heartbroken. It still hurts to this day. I suppose that's racing, you just have to knuckle down and get on with it. That's the nature of the sport; there are lots of ups and downs. That was a big downer that one.

Twelve months later and the complete reverse as I finally crossed the line in first place for my maiden TT win. Breaking the lap record was the icing on the cake. It was a fairly uneventful race as far as I was concerned. I started number three so didn't see too many people on the road which meant I could ride as I wanted to without any hindrance. Charlie Williams interviewed me in the winner's enclosure and asked what was going through my mind on the last lap. I replied that I opened the tank to see if I had enough fuel! As a child I had dreamt about racing at the TT but to win a race there was beyond my wildest dreams, it really was something else. It was so important and I don't mind admitting to being a little emotional. Mick Mooney was elderly by then so to give him a TT win was something special because he was such a great sponsor as well as a great friend. The only fly in the ointment was that he wasn't allowed into the winner's enclosure. Having raced at the TT in the 1950s he knew what it meant to win so it was a shame he couldn't share the moment with me.

For 1986 I'd wanted to keep my racing to a minimum so just concentrated on trying to retain my TT F2 World Championship title. I was still overcoming my broken femur and still had the massive pin in my leg. The prize money for the TT Formula Two World championship was very good, you were paid for qualifying and starting plus a big financial incentive for winning. I retained my title and it was full steam ahead for 1987 or so it seemed. We were at the FIM Congress for the prize presentation and there was a lot of talk about extending the TT Formula World championship to eight rounds including one at Donington Park. That was on the first day and everything sounded fantastic, we had a bike and we were going for the hat-trick. The next day we walked in to be met by the journalist Norrie Whyte who broke the news that they'd decided to scrap the Formula 2 championship altogether. We couldn't believe it. That was a big disappointment. With no World title to retain, the '87 season felt very flat.

I'd also been contacted by Honda Britain who wanted to know if I'd signed for anybody for 1987. I said I hadn't so they asked if I would consider signing for them to which I replied *'definitely, yes!'* They'd been a dominant force in racing and had run the likes of Phil Read, Ron Haslam, Joey Dunlop and Wayne Gardner. They offered me the RVF, the 3-cylin-

"As a child I had dreamt about racing at the TT but to win a race there was beyond my wildest dreams, it really was something else."

BRIAN REID

der 500, the Honda 250, every bike under the sun plus I would have full Rothmans backing and I would run the team from Ireland. Then I asked about what would happen to Joey but they said not to worry about him, this is a separate thing, it would be my own team. I wanted to know what championships they expected me to do to which they replied it was up to me. If I wanted to do the TT Formula One World championship then I could. They added that the deal had been okayed by the Japanese, I just had to leave it a couple of weeks and then come across to meet the top Honda brass to sign the contract. I came off the phone scarcely believing what I'd just been told. Then one morning I bought the local paper and the headline on the back page was '*Honda Britain disbands*.' I couldn't believe it. I was straight on the phone to them, a girl answered and she confirmed it was true, the team was no more. She added when they arrived for work that morning the gates were locked and they couldn't get in. It was the first any of the staff knew of it. She was eventually allowed in to answer the phones and I'll never forget while we were talking she burst into tears. I felt like crying too. With the TT Formula 2 championship being dropped and now this, it really felt like a kick in the teeth. It turned out that things became too expensive for Honda UK. Bike sales were down and while the amount of support they would get for the Formula 1 championship was good they couldn't come up with the backing for other racing. They still had their Rothmans sponsorship but Honda UK couldn't come up with the rest of the money needed.

I never tried to get too friendly with any of my rivals. I mainly kept myself to myself but I was always up for a bit of chat with Joey. He could be quiet too. Even if he knew you he would often walk past and not speak. He was the TT F1 champion and I the F2 that first year I won it and when we went to Estoril in Portugal to receive our gold medals we had to take a coach journey for the presentation. So I'm standing waiting to get on board when he walked up and carried on past me without saying a word. I thought,

'Great, here we both are hundreds of miles from home and he won't even speak to me.'

I boarded, found myself a seat and sat there for a few moments, next thing he got up from where he was sitting, placed himself next to me and started talking away. After the presentation we went back to the hotel, plonked ourselves at the bar and drank and laughed and joked until the sun came up the following morning.

1987 was also the year one of my great rivals began to make an impression on the road racing scene. I was riding the EMC bike at the Isle of Man and in the Junior TT there were damp conditions for the first couple of laps so I was being over cautious. This was the race when Steve Hislop announced himself to the world. He was leading by a fair distance until he retired leaving Eddie Laycock and myself to battle for the win and maybe, had I not been too careful to begin with, then I could have claimed the victory but as it was I had to settle for the runner-up spot by a couple of seconds. Another case of '*what if*?'

The next race was the Formula 2 and having missed out in the Junior I was really determined to win this one and was leading by eleven seconds at the end of the first lap. Hislop was in second place but took over top spot when my brand new ignition failed. By my reckoning, ignition failures have cost me three TT wins. So, we dumped the Hitachi ignition, replaced it with a German Kröber ignition and never had any trouble in that area ever again. I'd raced against Steve Hislop before and beat him at the Ulster Grand Prix but this year he really came to the fore. I met him at the TT prize giving and spent a bit of time with him then but it wasn't until I retired that we became really friendly

The first night of practice for TT88 I broke my toe. I was riding a 750 Kawasaki for Colin Aldridge and was going through the Kerrowmoar area where the road is very bumpy when my right foot jumped off the footrest, got trapped underneath and banged down hard on the road. I looked down and saw my boot was ripped to pieces. My first thought was I'd lost my toes! The cold air was rushing in so I couldn't feel them as I toured back to the paddock. I couldn't even bear to look down, I just kept thinking to myself '*My God, what have I done?*'

As soon as I got back I sat in my van and took off the boot, thankfully nothing was missing but my big toe was in a right mess. Shortly after my whole leg went black so I took a trip to the hospital where they x-rayed my foot and discovered I'd shattered the bones in my big toe.

I was still determined to ride so a pal of mine found a size nine boot which was bigger than what I would normally have worn as I was a seven. He took it to a cobbler who removed the sole so it opened out therefore allowing my swollen foot to fit inside but the biggest problem was that I used a right foot gear lever. Therefore I had to move it to the other side of the bike so I could use my left leg to change gear which I'd never done before but now my right foot kept catching the road because my new boot was so bulky. Somehow it all came together and I finished third in the Production race. I was leading the Junior and having a great scrap with Joey but my boot kept hitting the ground which gave me a few scares. I had to settle myself down, reduce my speed to make sure I made it to the finish, which was disappointing but on the other hand something of a bonus considering at one stage I didn't think I was going to be able to ride at all. Even though I was in agony and limping around the paddock I didn't take any painkillers, I don't like using them. I'd rather work my way through it. I finished second behind Joey which made the pain worthwhile.

I won the Supersport race at the NorthWest 200 in 1989 by beating Steve Hislop, Dave Leach and Jim Moodie and then jumped on the RC 30 for the next outing. I didn't last too long though as I tangled with someone on the first lap, fell and broke my collarbone. I went to the hospital and had it x-rayed where the doctor said there was nothing wrong, it wasn't broken but it didn't feel that way to me. However, he said the words I wanted to hear so I went to the TT a week or so later, did minimum practice and then tried to ride in the 600 race but didn't last long as the pain was terrible; it felt like an explosion going off in my shoulder when I tugged on the bars. I pulled in, retired and never rode again that week. Meanwhile, I went to Noble's hospital in Douglas where I had another x-ray which confirmed that my collarbone was indeed broken. One ray of light was Yamaha approaching me to see if I would ride for them next season. They had the backing of Budweiser and a good team in place so I quickly agreed a deal.

The Supersport 600 class was highly contested at this time, it was a class everyone really wanted to win. Honda and Yamaha were the two big rivals in this category and there were plenty of top guys taking part especially at the TT. It had now been four years since my one and only victory in the Isle of Man but that changed in the Supersport 600 race. Dave Leach led early on until his bike blew. I'd started at number three so things were fairly uneventful as far as I was concerned. I took over at the front, I didn't see too many people on the road and was getting good signals so I knew I had a decent enough lead while the Budweiser Yamaha felt comfortable; I didn't have to push. So I took the chequered flag and it felt great to be a TT winner again after what felt like such a long time. I needed to as well as Yamaha wanted to see results especially being backed by a multinational company. I was up against some proper talent in Johnny Rea, Steve Cull and Mark Farmer so I felt very good.

It looked like I would add to my TT victory tally in 1991 but that turned out to be a miserable year. In the Junior TT myself, Robert Dunlop and Phillip McCallen we're all very close together, we're talking a couple of seconds or so throughout the whole race. On the last lap I went into Handleys as usual, flicked left then right but for some reason on the exit I couldn't turn the bike. I could see the banking coming towards me, there was no way I was going to avoid it yet I seemed to have time to think about what was going on which was a realisation that I was going down. It felt like an eternity as everything seemed to be happening in slow motion until I slammed into it. A very quick place to go down. I was on the road for a long time. Joey came past, he'd slowed right down into first gear, I was there lying there staring up at him and our eyes met as he was looking down at me as he rode by. Up until that point the season was going incredibly well and I'd arrived at the TT leading seven championships. As I waited for the helicopter and I was in a lot of pain I thought to myself '*Well, that's that lot gone!*' I then decided I was done with racing. I just said *'What the hell am I doing? I can't be carrying on like this any-*

more. This isn't good.' Lying there in the road I was finished as far as I was concerned. I took the helicopter to have operations on my ankle and my arm which had both broken. My whole upper body was sore and I was in a lot of pain for a long time. Meanwhile, we discovered the linkage arm underneath the suspension was cracked which in turn broke the back end which is why I couldn't turn it. I eventually left hospital but was lying around at home, I couldn't move much and when I did it was with the aid of crutches. The Ulster Grand Prix was coming up when my mechanic called to see me. I asked if he could bring my 400 from the garage to see if I could ride it. I managed to get on and ride it up and down the road; it felt brilliant! I decided to race it at the Ulster if the authorities would let me which they did so I threw the crutches away, went to Dundrod and rode the 400 to a podium finish. I went on to win a few more races before the end of the season. I don't know how I managed to do so with a broken leg but somehow I did. Maybe I was just determined to finish off the season by winning and therefore knowing I was back on form again before the start of the following year. The final race of the campaign was at Nutts Corner and I managed to beat Dave Leach in a terrific battle, he really was tough to beat. It was a great way to end a mixed season.

I didn't begin 1992 too brightly, both the Yamaha 600 and 400 machines just weren't on the pace. When we tried to find out why, my guy who worked on the motors just shrugged his shoulders. We were way down on speed. To compound matters I asked Yamaha for a 250 but they said I couldn't have one. I was seriously contemplating not going to the TT that year because the bikes were so bad. I asked V&M if they could supply me with an engine yet what they were asking was out of my price range plus I would have to supply all the parts and the biggest problem of all was they wouldn't have time to build it. The situation changed a couple of days later when they called me to say they knew where there was one of their 400s sitting around doing nothing, I just had to ring a guy called Phil Connolly to see if I could use it. So I rang him, he'd never heard of me, road racing and the TT just wasn't his thing so he was very dubious about me but agreed he'd have someone bring the bike on the understanding I wasn't allowed to touch it. They would do all the work on it which suited me fine. At the same time, I had a phone call from Yamaha to say they had Steve Hislop's Loctite 250 available. He was due to ride it but there'd been some sort of fall out between them and he'd switched to Padgetts so now the bike was available for me if i wanted. All of a sudden, my TT was back on.

The first race was the 400. Carl Fogarty was riding the V&M bike and he stormed practice putting in a best lap of 112mph; nobody else was anywhere near. My best was something like 108mph so I didn't have much hope as he was miles faster than anybody. We started the race and I put in 112mph from a standing start to break the lap record with Foggy very close in second, there wasn't much in it. After the pitstop I had a signal saying he was out and my lead shot up to 50 seconds or so. That meant I could just bring it home, which I did, to win eventually by over a minute ahead of Philip McCallen. Two days before the race I had met Phil Connolly for the first time and from his being dubious with me he was now over the moon. He couldn't believe he had a TT winning bike.

In the 400 race when I got to my first board it had said '*P1 +1*' so when I set off on my Loctite bike in the Junior race and approached the sign this time I was thinking '*Please give me the same signal, please be one plus one*'. It was actually even better as the first board read '*P1 +2*'. I was shouting in my head '*brilliant, brilliant!*' That motivated me to push harder. Now normally I would have had my own guys in the pits but Yamaha insisted I use their crew. So I came in for my stop with an eleven second lead over Steve Hislop in second place. Things were going well until the guy on the fuel pulled out the nozzle and soaked me and the bike with about half a gallon of petrol. It was everywhere. Then we tried to start the bike but it refused. They tried to push me off and the bike made that '*bubble, bubble, bubble*' noise but wouldn't chime in. The crew walked away as I rolled down the pitlane and just as I got to the end the bike fired up. When I reached Quarterbridge I hit the brakes but they weren't working as the fuel had soaked the callipers in the pads. I ran straight on and went left instead of right so then I had to turn the bike around. This was costing me valuable time. My lead was wiped out and my next board said *'zero'*. Not only that, the events had really messed with my head. Somehow, I kept it together and started to build the lead back up again so much so I soon saw a sign saying *'plus ten seconds'*. Don't forget I was up against Steve Hislop and he was soon closing down the gap. As I started my last lap my board there said '*plus six*'. He was definitely coming back at me. I arrived at the Gooseneck and the signal was now '*P2 -1*' that was second minus a second. I'd lost the lead of the race. So I just said to myself, *'I'm not losing this.'* Over the Mountain, I was balls out, going into corners much harder than I've ever done before, really pushing the envelope so to speak. Everything was working great. I dropped down into Douglas and crossed the line. I had started at number five while Steve was nineteen so I had to wait for him to cross the line. When I pulled into the winners enclosure, the guy put up two fingers at me to say I had finished second. I didn't realise at the time but he couldn't have known the result yet I was totally disheartened having led the race twice by a good margin then riding like I'd never rode before over the Mountain. So we stood there waiting for a minute or two, I couldn't hear the circuit commentary but people all around me were listening to the radio when suddenly there was a loud cheer. Hizzy had finished but I couldn't believe it, I'd won by 3.2 seconds so I had pulled 4.2 seconds over the mountain on the last lap. On the podium Steve turned to me and said

"I don't know how you did that? I was on the limit."

When he came in to finish the race he had grass and mud on the footrest where he had hit the bank at Keppel Gate so he had been trying too. He always said he wanted to win the Junior so he was a bit disappointed to say the least. As it turned out it would be the only major TT honour he never won. I was elated especially surrounding the circumstances because it was Steve Hislop, because it was Loctite Yamaha, because I had been leading and lost the lead and then when I finished not knowing if I'd won. It was all those things that made it special.

I also made a good friend in Adrian Marsh. He was working for Loctite Yamaha and we got on brilliantly together. This was also the year of

Steve Hislop's win on the Norton, a race I missed out on as my bike was broken. I watched at the start and finish and I saw Steve wobbling his way through at high speed and thought to myself '*how is he doing that?*' It looked horrendous to handle. When I won the 250 race Foggy was jumping up and down, he was over the moon hugging me as we were Loctite teammates along with Mark Farmer. So because he'd supported me I was supporting him in the Senior but because I was friendly with Steve it was a bit difficult to know where my loyalties were. As it turned out Steve won the race and Carl broke the lap record. So wins all round as far as I was concerned.

I loved the Loctite Yamaha in 1992, it did everything right. Lovely to ride. I wish the same could be said of the '93 bike. This was totally the opposite, I couldn't get it to handle at all. We tried the same suspension setup as before, everything was the same yet it wanted to shake its head and wobble all the time. We struggled with it at home in Northern Ireland and at the TT, spending practice week trying to sort out the handling problems. We took it up to the Dyno and tried everything, working on different cylinders but the situation remained hopeless. I didn't have much confidence in the bike as I set off along Glencrutchery Road and then to make matters worse my tear-offs ripped open halfway down Bray Hill. They didn't blow off completely, just ripped down the middle so I was looking through part tear off, part visor. I rode out to Ballacraine almost with one hand trying to rip the whole thing off but with dirty, oily gloves I couldn't get a good enough grip. Before the race started I'd been very nervous, much more than normal, so I wasn't feeling too optimistic as I approached my first board. I felt I'd lost a lot of time struggling with the tear off so imagine my surprise when I got there to find out I'm leading the race. There's a small road on the left coming out of Kirk Michael just before Rhen Cullen and that's where my signaller would position himself. I'd started at five again with the Dunlops, Joey and Robert, at three and four respectively. Joey wouldn't let me go and came by so from then on we kept passing each other. However, his constant being there was sort of upsetting me as Jim Moodie was my biggest threat. I had a cushion of around seven seconds, something like that and I was afraid Joey could mess it up for me. His bike was a wee bit better than mine so would come flying past me down every straight. I wanted a clear road but couldn't get it. Going over the mountain on the last lap, I actually looked around and waved at him to stay behind me. I don't know how well that went down at the time but I knew I was leading and I needed nothing in front of me. I was dreading him coming past me once more. Joey understood though and stayed behind me all the way to the chequered flag as I took the win. Afterwards I was sat with him when he said

"My, that bike of yours is a flying machine."

"You're winding me up," I replied.

"No, no," said Joey. *"Your bike is better than mine."*

"I'll tell you what then Joey, we'll do a swap."

That's where the conversation ended!

I'd been riding Winston McAdoo's 600 from time to time but in 1994 we struck up a deal so he bought a 250 to go with the Supersport bike. Adrian Marsh was still working for me and we got a deal for Michelin tyres. My two previous Junior TT wins were on Dunlops but I had to buy their rubber as they wouldn't supply free ones for the race. That had pissed me off a bit. The trouble was even though I wasn't paying for them I didn't get on too well with the Michelins. The rear was good yet the front wouldn't go where I wanted it to on the road as daft as that sounds. I convinced myself it would be fine but it just didn't work out so I had to settle for second behind Joey. If you look at the history books you'll see that Joey rode at six that day instead of his favoured number three. There's a good reason for this. I'd sent in my entry for the TT that year but never got a reply. I waited and waited but heard nothing. Time was ticking so I got in touch with the organisers who told me they'd not received anything from me so therefore assumed I wasn't coming. I confirmed I was going and asked if I could ride at number five as I had done in previous years only to be told

"I'm sorry but five has gone"

"Well, do you have any numbers available in the top ten?"

"Yes, seven is available."

"Brilliant. That'll do me."

A while later, Davey Wood asked if I had my numbers for the TT. When I told him I was going at seven his face dropped. He explained he and Joey went to number six so they would start ten seconds behind me as they thought I'd be at five! Their plan had backfired. Some smart-arse journalist said I'd changed my number so I was 10 seconds behind Joey but the truth was I didn't even know he had changed from his usual three.

As it turned out it wasn't a memorable race. On one hand I was happy enough to finish second considering the way the bike was but on the other I was disappointed as I knew I was capable of winning if things had been right.

Shortly after the TT I raced at Skerries in Ireland. A few days later I had a call from my uncle Ian who'd been down there watching me and asked if I'd enjoyed it to which I replied I hadn't really. He then suggested that maybe I packed it in but I explained I couldn't even if I wanted to. I felt I'd be letting people down if I did. He suspected I'd lost a bit of motivation and told me it didn't matter about anyone else; when it's time, it's time. Winston McAdoo wanted to buy a new bike for the Ulster Grand Prix which I wanted to ride. Ian said I should do that but then that's it, you're finished. I knew what he was saying was correct. He was always on the money when it came to advice. Before the Ulster was the Temple 100 and I felt at home on the bike. I started the race on the 600 feeling very comfortable, taking things steady and was in third place when I decided I was going to start the next lap by going for it. That never happened as Ian King crashed in front of me which I couldn't avoid, He was killed and I was badly injured. This happened at 130mph. I broke almost every bone in my body. I was lucky to survive it, Ian wasn't so fortunate. That was the end of my racing career. The only consolation, if you could call it that, was that it hadn't been my fault. I toyed with the idea about making a comeback and it tortured me for years. I considered riding a 250 at the TT, just for the joy of it but common sense kicked in and I stayed away.

As I recuperated I was wondering what the hell am I gonna do now? I missed the racing, mostly the involvement away from the racetrack, the phone calls, which just stopped overnight. When it did eventually ring it was a guy I was friendly with and he asked me to become involved with him as he had an outside broadcast truck. So we became partners and began covering events like the Ulster Grand Prix and other races for TV. So I found myself back in racing again and did that for a while before moving onto other things.

I do love going back to the Isle of Man to watch the TT. It's the one race I miss and there's nothing better than being asked to take part in a parade lap. I can't describe how fantastic it is when you get out there and you feel like you're back, riding around again. It is such a special feeling to zip around the TT circuit.

After a couple of roles involving satellite and computer systems as well as an electronics company Brian now lives in retirement with his wife. They have two sons, Mark who works in security and has a black belt in Krav Maga while Simon has followed in his father's footsteps as a motorcycle racer and is a regular competitor in the British championship. Brian can often be found spectating at many motorcycle road racing events in the Isle of Man or Northern Ireland

IAN SIMPSON

Born Dalbeattie, Scotland

TT Years 1989, 1993-94, 1996-98
21 races, 3 x wins, 3 x 2nd, 2 x 3rd, 3 x 4th, 1 x 5th, 2 x 7th, 1 x 10th, 1 x 12th 1 x 15th, 1 x 26th, 3 x DNF

MGP 1987-88
1 x 2nd, 1 x 12th, 2 x DNF

Ian Simpson, the son of a TT winner, went on to emulate his father Bill three times in the Isle of Man and may have added considerably to that total had his career not been cut short by injury, his five British championship titles achieved on short circuits a testament to that. His TT debut came in one of the darkest years of the event's history and he then took time out from the Island for a while before making an instant impact on his return in the mid-90s. Podium placings were soon followed by victories, his last race being the Senior TT, which he won. Away from the Isle of Man he won the Superbike class of the British Supercup the year before it became BSB along with the 600cc title as well.

My Grandad was a doctor at racetracks in southern Africa and his son, my Dad's older brother, started racing and that's how our family motorsport story began. They'd moved to Rhodesia, which is now known as

Zimbabwe, from Scotland at a time when my father and his brother were very young. They stayed out there for around a dozen years or so before returning to the UK. Dad became a racer, met my Mum and had me so all my earliest memories centre around racing. All the way through school, when asked what I'd become when I grew up, I told everyone I was going to be a motorbike racer. My response was usually met with

"No, really, what are you going to do?"

I was determined though so that's what happened when I turned sixteen and got out on track for the first time, however, for the first couple of years I didn't have my father's support. He tried to talk me out of it, saying I'd hurt myself and how it was very difficult to pursue a career in racing. I stuck at it though and eventually started to improve so he began turning up at race meetings, which was a massive boost as he helped out enormously.

Dad raced and won at the TT so as a family we were always in the Isle of Man come June each year. I believe I've missed just one since I was born so it's always been a part of my life. We'd often stay at the Sandringham Hotel in Douglas, which was run by Dave and Joyce Bridge who went on to become my first ever sponsor. They were so much fun to be around and stuck by me in my early days when I was fairly hopeless. As a child I'd often be running around the paddock pestering the riders for autographs and somewhere I still have my book with signatures from Mike Hailwood, Phil Read, Steve Tonkin, Jon Ekerold, in fact everybody and anybody is in there. There'd be the odd one who would snub you and that hurt so I always made a point when I was older to never refuse a request for an autograph. There are photos which my Granny took of me playing football with Mike Hailwood and Alex George around the back of the Grandstand in 1978. There are more pictures of me than them; I'm certain she didn't know who or how famous they were. Still, it's a cool thing to have; not many can say they've had a kickabout with Mike Hailwood.

I've always been a proper TT fan, I've never been one of those competitors who just wanted to race motorbikes. If there are bikes on TV then I'm watching whether it's qualifying for MotoGP or a TT DVD, I don't mind being labelled as a real anorak. When my Dad raced in the Isle of Man I was always up at the Grandstand but since I retired I've always gone to watch somewhere on the course. By my reckoning there's only a couple of places I've not been to. I don't think there are too many who can say that. I've been at every corner, many of which you probably couldn't do now since viewing restrictions came in. I still haven't watched at Handley's; another spot is the kink in the road where the bikes wheelie just after Kerrowmoar. I can't think of any other places I've not spectated from. Many times I've taken a trials bike with pals, gone off-road over the Mountain and been to every vantage point there. I've discussed this with John McGuinness and even he can't think of any spot I've not been to when we've gone through the list. One of my favourite places is at the end of the Mountain mile; that sorts the men out from the boys. There's a drainage ditch under the road so you can position yourself on the outside of the track to watch from and if you move along a bit there's the triple left hander at the Mountain Box which is another great point to see the quick guys go through.

I also like to go where you see riders do things differently. Places like Creg ny Baa are not that spectacular where everyone goes down four gears, brakes, turns and then on their way again whereas somewhere like the 33rd milestone you can see John McGuinness come down a gear earlier than everyone else. When I mentioned it to him he was amazed I'd noticed. Bruce Anstey at Appledene has slightly different lines to anyone else through there. You can learn so much if you know what you're looking for. Michael Rutter would always seek my advice about how his machine was behaving because I like looking for whether bikes are too stiff or too soft and quite often you notice they've too much traction control which is slowing them down so therefore needs switching off. I enjoy the different styles between riders too, John McGuinness is a fine example. He would often be sitting up on the bike with his head high and he'd be doing that to make it more stable. I've often heard people say his motorcycle handles much better than anyone else's but I'd then point out it's not his bike, it's him that's doing that. Then you'd hear that Guy Martin's bike looks unstable as it's all over the place and again I'm saying that's his riding style, nothing to do with the bike. He'd be rushing in and shutting the throttle at the last moment, loading up the front and by this point I'm peering through my fingers fearing the worst. One of the best I've seen is Steve Plater. I was at the Bungalow in 2009 when he won the Senior, setting new sector records over the Mountain at the time. He was the fastest rider I've ever seen through one corner; he must have been around ten miles an hour faster than anyone else who came through there that day. He was two-wheel drifting through the corner, using every inch of the road, it was utter perfection. When he says he was trying hard on that last lap then you better believe it.

I got to ride with Steve in a parade lap at the TT and it was simply the best time I've had. I set off first, he followed me to Ramsey at which point he went past and I followed him over the Mountain, the pair of us going far too fast for a parade lap. I was on a Suzuki 1100 my Dad built and he was riding a Suzuki 750. When we came in we were grinning like idiots. I told him I was glad he didn't go any faster than he had been and he was saying the same about me. It really was incredible fun.

My first time on the Mountain course came in 1987 at the Manx Grand Prix where I finished second in the Lightweight Newcomers race on a Yamaha TZR 250. The following year in the Senior I was dicing with eventual winner Paul Hunt and Phil Hogg until he crashed out while my race came to an end when my Suzuki 1100 sprang a fuel leak. I also fell off at Ballacraine in the Junior on a TZ350 so while it was good fun it wasn't very successful.

I decided not to return to the Manx in 1989 as I felt I was ready for the TT but that year turned out to be a horrendous experience. Phil Mellor was my team-mate at Durex Suzuki and all through the season he'd been more than helpful towards me, offering tips which was making me improve and even though I was beating him from time to time on the short circuits he was still there for me, offering advice when others may not have been so quick in coming forward. I had so much time and respect for Mez. He was such a lovely, genuine, warm, funny person with a very good sense of humour and would constantly have us all in stitches. It was very hard to come to terms with when he died in the Production 1300 TT on the same lap that claimed one of my Dad"s good friends, Steve Henshaw. I also lost a good pal when Phil Hogg was killed during practice. I firmly believe he would have gone on to win a few TTs. In the space of a few days there'd been three fatalities of whom I knew each one very well so I just decided the TT was no longer for me and wouldn't race there anymore.

Maybe there's something in the saying that time's a great healer because I eventually changed my mind and decided to go back to compete in 1993 and again in '94 but that year Mark Farmer was killed which really upset me and I know Jim Moodie felt the same; all three of us were close pals. Mark was such a fast, controlled rider which made his death so much more of a shock. It brought home that if it could happen to someone as good as him then it could happen to anybody. It really affected me so I stayed away again in 1995. Even though racing at the TT was the best experience I'd ever had I was always more than aware of the danger and simply didn't want to die there. I must be honest and admit there were plenty of times when I was terrified riding around. I'm sure others feel the same and maybe don't admit it. It wasn't so bad if you had a nice 600 or something similar but some of the Superbikes and big production machines were just horrendously dangerous and difficult to control especially when they didn't know which way they wanted to go.

Learning the TT course is a massive undertaking. Before I raced there my Dad would take me around in the van and give me loads of tips plus I used to pester Steve Hislop for advice at every opportunity. I'd bundle Hizzy into a car and we'd go for a lap. He'd point out things which you'd take in as there was no better person to listen to. For me, he was the best rider ever at the TT. Without a shadow of a doubt. He was special. In the British Superbike championship he would be on record breaking pace by lap three of the first free practice session which nobody else ever did, it was almost impossible. I reckon if there was a BSB race without any practice and everyone just jumped on their bike and raced then Steve would have won every one and by about half a lap. He had a natural feel and ability to read roads and circuits which I've never seen anybody do. It was the same at the Isle of Man TT. Even if he didn't get as much practice for whatever reason it wouldn't bother him in the slightest to just jump on a bike and immediately be on the pace. Bizarrely, it seemed he didn't need any practice and the more time he spent qualifying, the more he seemed to get fed up with it and would lose interest to the point where I feel it actually slowed him down. One time we were at the Almeria track in Spain where he rode Stuart Easton's Ducati 748. We were coming to the end of the final session and I suggested to Steve he should have a go of Stuart's bike particularly as he'd never ridden a 748 before. Well, immediately he was on it. He only did something like four laps but was already inside the lap record; Stuart just looked at me and said

"I've been here for three days getting the hang of that bike and Steve's just smoked my time. That's it, I'm retiring!"

Don't forget Stuart was such a good rider too, there weren't many who could go quicker than him plus he was a worthy British champion. Steve should have achieved so much more than he did. At times he seemed as if he wasn't interested in racing, on other occasions I believe he would perhaps think about things too much and could be easily upset by something that someone said. Characters like Jim Moodie or Michael Rutter would just ignore anything like criticism whereas Steve would take a lot of stuff to heart and that could affect him.

I certainly had no better teacher than Steve at the TT. I still remember the things he taught me. Coming out of Glen Helen he'd suggest to follow the line as it would straighten you as you went up the hill. I see some riders going through there nowadays doing it totally wrong. Another is Doran's where you hug the bank and go down the right hand side as you come out of the bend and you see riders swerving all over the place but Steve had it sussed. I remember everything he told me

"Hug in tight here, don't let the bike drift out there, you need to be on that part of the road"

I still use his tips today if I'm doing a parade lap. These were things that didn't seem that obvious. Today, you see experienced TT riders being in the wrong bit of the road. I know things have changed a bit now with Superbikes being so powerful that you square up a bit more and straighten things out a little bit than you used to so there are lines that are no longer there. Steve would also use all of the road at a time when the bikes didn't handle as well plus the tyres were nowhere near as good as they are today. If you put modern rubber on my old bikes they handle so much better than when I raced them. Michael Rutter and myself were black and blue all up our arms and legs at the TT in 1998 from hanging on to the RC45s. You couldn't even hold them flat out in a straight line; they were that unstable. You look at Steve Hislop's lines on the RC45 in 1994 when he won both big bike races, that machine would have been so tough to control using those tyres. He couldn't take off and lean over, he had to square off every single rise in the road to make sure the bike stayed upright with the wheels in line. If they weren't then he'd be straight through the hedge. So there are different lines and techniques used today which differ from my time there because some things have changed. Another example is through Union Mills where the bikes are leant over on their side with both wheels on the ground. In my day you wouldn't have done that because back then you would have been picking the bike up at that point so when it takes off it's upright and heading in the right direction. I don't think you ever stop learning at the TT. On every lap you pick things up. When I first went I had a good idea where I was going even before my first practice session because I'd been to so many races there and if anyone was going for a lap in a van or a car I'd jump in with them. There's a story that Joey Dunlop said on his first time at the TT he didn't know whether to go left, right or straight on at Ballacraine. I never had that problem.

Maybe I worried too much at the TT. I see the likes of John McGuinness and I believe part of the reason he has won so many is that he stays calm. If he's on a bike that he knows isn't going to win then he'll just bring it home and not push when there's no need to. Honda always wanted me

"If you don't like a bike, if it doesn't work for you, if it's slow, if it doesn't handle how you want, if it doesn't suit you then you shouldn't ride it as I found out to my cost."

IAN SIMPSON

to ride Fireblades in the Production race but I just hated them with a passion. I couldn't get on with them. They just felt horrible. I struggled to control them and even if I wasn't going too fast it still felt like I was going to ditch it. Some bikes you can ride the wheels off, go extremely quick and never feel that you're gonna crash. I was never comfortable finishing seventh or twelfth on a bike I wasn't happy with, that would really annoy me so I'd still push. It sounds aloof but I felt I was getting beaten by riders that I should be beating. That probably shortened my career as I was crashing through trying too hard and hurting myself badly in the process whereas I should have left it until the next race, the next meeting, the next year. If you don't like a bike, if it doesn't work for you, if it's slow, if it doesn't handle how you want, if it doesn't suit you then you shouldn't ride it as I found out to my cost. There were times when I dug deep for wins I probably shouldn't have won.

Even though there were years when I decided not to race at the TT I still went along to watch with the likes of James Whitham, I was still in love with the racing and I was seeing riders getting good results which had me thinking I could have given them a race. There were guys I was beating on short circuits in the British championship and they were going on to win TTs. I still wanted to win one, as I always had done, and thought if I did manage to do so then that would do me, I would call it a day having achieved my ambition. When I went back in 1993 I did okay, going well in the Formula One race until the bike suffered a misfire. I came into the pits and my Dad discovered a loose wire in the coil. It took about 10 minutes to fix it so I'd lost a lot of time. I decided to carry on to test it and make sure it was working perfectly. I ended up near the bottom of the leaderboard but I knew the bike was fine.

I took my first podium in the Supersport 600; that was a good race. I finished second to Iain Duffus who beat me fair and square but maybe I would have taken the victory had both of my contact lenses not blown out coming over the mountain. At that point I had a good lead of something like five seconds but being short-sighted I was struggling with my visibility and began to slow. Iain pulled something like fifteen seconds on me over two sectors. Fortunately, I was running at number nine and he was number ten so when he eventually passed me I was able to tuck in behind and follow him around even if he was something of a blur. I knew there was no chance of me taking the win so therefore a second place was a great result considering the circumstances, struggling to make out where I was going. It's hard to pick out apexes and lines when you can't see properly. The same thing would happen in reverse for me in the Formula One TT in 1998 when Michael Rutter was leading when his contact lens slipped and I ended up winning by a couple of seconds. I probably would have won the 600 race and Michael the F1 had our vision not been impaired on each occasion.

Having not ridden at the TT in 1995 following Mark Farmer's death I wasn't actually meant to take part in '96 until Mike Edwards, who was due to ride for V&M, injured himself so Jack Valentine called and asked if I would take over. This was about a week before practice had begun. I knew Jack and Steve Mellor who ran the team, it was a proper set-up but still you needed a good sense of humour to be part of the squad. They were a good bunch of lads who knew when to work and when to laugh. As it was I only had a 600 and a production bike for the TT because that was all Mike was due to ride. I finished third in the Junior. That was a good bike to ride but again, I never felt at home with the Fireblade, my best result on that was tenth in the Senior.

I stayed with V&M for 1997. The year before I'd never ridden the bike beforehand but managed a podium finish on that occasion, this time I was doing a full British Supersport championship season so was on the 600 week in, week out before that year's TT. This was my ride this time, not somebody else's so I had it set up exactly as I liked it. I'm very fussy about how my bikes are so that means the handlebars have to be the exact length that I want and the same with the levers, gear stick and foot pegs plus the seat has to be completely flat. For the big classes I had a RC45 but unlike the 600 it wasn't my bike, it had been somebody else's. Practice week went okay and I managed 117 mph on the Supersport machine. On race day everything just came together, I led from the start and set a new lap record of 119.86mph, just a shade off becoming the first guy to do 120 on a 600. My sector times from Ramsey to Ramsey were unofficially over the 120mph mark. I kept the lead all the way to the flag and created a new race record of 118.41mph. That stayed untouched for a few years which I'm very proud of especially as the later bikes were miles faster. A couple of years later I was watching at Kirk Michael as I'd broken my leg at Snetterton and was amazed by Dave Jefferies as he went on to win the 600 race. He looked so fast through there, him and Jim Moodie but they didn't break my record. Watching from the outside you never realise how quick you're actually going. It doesn't look anywhere near as fast when you're riding. Afterwards Jack said the new R6 that DJ was riding had about 15 horsepower more than I'd had two years earlier so I must have been going some.

So what did it feel like to win a TT? Having achieved a lifetime ambition it turned out to be something of an anticlimax in a way. After the race I went back to my van, sat there and thought *'is that it?'* It sounds terrible that I felt that way with it being everything I'd dreamed of but there I was sitting by myself, somewhat a little deflated. Once you've won one no-one can ever take that away from you though no matter how you feel. There's one deal I've unfortunately never kept and that was with my first sponsor Dave Bridge. Even when I was wobbling around at the Manx he said I'd go on to win a TT so I promised if I ever did I would take him to Macau. I've still not managed to take him but maybe one day.

1998 would be my last outing at the TT as a rider. I was with the Honda Britain team but this was effectively still V&M as the operation this season was run by Jack and Steve. Race week started well when I bagged my first big bike win at the TT in the Formula 1. Ray McCullough was watching me at Kerrowmoar and he said I was miles quicker through there than anyone else. There can be no greater praise than when it's from an Irish road racing legend. When he'd told me I felt like walking around with my chest out for the rest of the day. The race had been postponed from Saturday, the start was then delayed and the distance reduced from six to four laps. It was a very tough encounter, there were damp patches all over the place. Michael led for the first three laps until he had his contact lens issue so he slowed and I took the lead. The last lap was hairy as I had a cut slick tyre at the front and there were quite a few places still wet. I was really pushing and I remember thinking I could never do a lap at the TT like this again. It was one of those where your luck was going to run out sooner rather than later. Thankfully, it all held together and I won by just over two seconds from my team-mate and was just over a second off Carl Fogarty's lap record. I never fell off at the TT unlike the Manx where I tipped off at Ballacraine on my 350 and crashed my TZR at Windy Corner but this lap though could have been different.

Even though we were the official Honda team at the TT people would look at you from the outside and see big artics and team shirts so get the impression it's some massive operation yet really it was still me with my two childhood pals, Snowy and Keith, working on my bikes along with my Dad, the same little squad we'd had for years. As far removed from the glamorous looking world of people walking around in official gear trying to appear important but who wouldn't know one end of a motorcycle from the other.

The 600 race was another tricky affair. Michael Rutter started eighty seconds ahead of me on the road and for the opening three laps we'd been neck and neck on the leaderboard. I may have been in the lead going into the last lap when it started to rain yet because he was so far ahead of me he was getting dry roads whereas I wasn't so fortunate being further back on the course but that's the nature of the TT. There's nothing worse than when I've won a race and you hear somebody else's excuses for not winning. Had it stayed dry then who knows, it could have been a different outcome but as far as I'm concerned he won it fair and square. I pushed so hard on the final twenty miles or so in the rain and I remember coming in thinking if anybody else went quicker then they deserve it. As it happened Michael beat me by around a second or so.

I'll never forget being really confused by a pit board in the Senior race that year. I was at number three and thinking about who was going to be a major threat. I'd had a big lead until lap three when it disappeared.

I knew it wasn't Michael as he was out and it wasn't until I came in for my second stop at the end of lap four I was told Bob Jackson was doing a one-pit strategy coming in at the halfway point. Early on I'd slowed down a fair bit as I had such a good lead and thinking about bringing it home. By carrying on at the end of lap two, while I had pitted, Bob made up all that time. Unfortunately for him he lost it all as when he did come in for his stop the filler cap wouldn't go back on the tank properly after refuelling and they conceded valuable seconds trying to get it back into place. Had that not happened then I'm certain he would have won. I was cruising, if you could call it that, thinking I had it in the bag so therefore not over-revving the bike or taking any chances like I had done in the previous races. Had I been aware of his strategy beforehand then I'd have approached things differently. So I won the Senior but I really felt for Bob as he was such a good rider. Quite a few times at the North West 200 in Northern Ireland in the early 90s I couldn't believe how fast he was on a 600 considering he never raced on short circuits. There'd be me, Jim Moodie, Steve Ives, guys who were racing British championship on a regular basis whereas Bob turned up, rolled his bike out of the back of a van and then started banging elbows with us on the track. You can't have anything except total respect for him to be able to do that.

After Honda Britain in 1998 Jack and Steve started up V&M again the following year and I was to race for them once more, this time alongside Dave Jefferies. However it wasn't to be as, early in the season, I crashed coming out of the Bomb Hole at Snetterton and smashed my leg up. Having recovered from that I was due to race at the TT in 2000 but in the opening round of the British championship at Brands Hatch I went into the wall on the exit at Clearways and this time really hurt myself. I was in intensive care for a long time with broken embolisms, multiple fractures and at one stage they were going to cut my right leg off at the top and my left at the knee. Luckily they managed to save them but it did mean years and years of operations to have my leg straightened, lengthened and pointing in the right direction which is a small price to pay especially as I can now ride a bike again.

So that was me finished as a racer. I can remember lying at the side of the track at Brands Hatch knowing it had all come to an end. In a strange way it was something of a relief. I'd hurt myself so often and spent far too much time on crutches that I was really sick of it.

I then went into team management and did a few years with Dienza Ducati, ETI and ran Robbie Burns in BSB which was a lot of fun. That was the Vitrans team and the pair of us are still good pals and do the odd spot of classic racing together.

I still get out and about on a bike whenever I can. Iain MacPherson organises a trip every year, he seems to know every nook and cranny of Scotland and there's usually me, Brian Morrison, Jim Moodie, James Whitham, a whole load of us ex-racers who blip around for two or three days having a great time. I run a similar business taking people on biking tours around the Highlands, away from the usual tourist spots on some spectacular roads. Beautiful places many folk would never get to see. It may not be the same as racing but it's thoroughly enjoyable all the same.

I treasure all my time spent at the TT whether I was a child, a fan or a racer. I vividly remember being with my Dad at the top of Barregarrow in the early 80s and Graeme McGregor was the first bike due on the road. We were waiting for the race to start and sat on the banking where you're not allowed to go now. At that time I was riding bikes every day be it in the woods with my pals or fields somewhere back home. I remember looking at the corner thinking '*He will come through here, maybe go down a couple of gears then drop down toward the bottom of the hill.*' I was also going to a lot of short circuits with my Dad at the time so had a grasp of what to expect. As we sat there waiting I could hear a 350 in the distance, approaching flat out, that two-stroke whine bouncing off the sides of the road for a couple of miles as it screamed towards us. It grew closer then next thing '*whoosh*' he went past without shutting off. I was gobsmacked. I can still picture Graeme in the George Beale colours, the blue 350 plate with number one on it and his yellow and red helmet. I'd never seen anything like it in my life. From that moment I was hooked.

Ian still lives in Dalbeattie having invested in property both residential and business. He runs his own tour company Adventure Moto Scotland which offers trips both home and abroad. He has one daughter, Hannah.

MURRAY WALKER

son of Graham Walker

Born Birmingham, England
Graham born Wallington, England

Graham's TT Years 1920-1934
1 x win, 3 x 2nd, 2 x 3rd, 1 x 4th, 5 x 5th, 2 x 6th, 1 x 10th, 1 x 13th, 8 x DNF

Murray Walker is known to millions worldwide as the voice of Formula One racing yet his broadcasting career began with plenty of focus on motorcycle racing in particular the Isle of Man TT where his father Graham had raced. They would team up as the commentary team for the BBC's coverage of the event with Murray taking over the lead role from his dad when he died in 1962. He would continue in that position until the British Grand Prix switched from the Island to Silverstone in 1977. Despite not returning for many years he often spoke of his love for the Isle of Man TT.

I first went to the Isle of Man when I was two-years-old in my mother's arms because my dad raced there. He first competed in 1920 and every year thereafter until 1935. He wasn't exactly the Geoff Duke of his day, but he wasn't very far off because he won the TT and had umpteen places. He was a works rider for Norton and then Sunbeam, subsequently going to Rudge Whitworth where he made his name really. He won the Lightweight TT, was second in the Senior and so I grew up going to the Isle of Man because I always went during school holidays with my parents. Any recollections I give now are from before the war and obviously those of a child who's growing up, and not from someone who took part in the TT. That's one of my great ambitions that wasn't ever realised and will never be realised. I used to race bikes after the war, but I was never good enough to satisfy myself and I was certainly never good enough to ride in the TT. So my recollections begin with staying at the Castle Mona hotel on the seafront in Douglas. Then it was the place to stay because although it's not generally known, the Castle Mona hotel was the ancestral home of the Derby family. Allegedly, the Derby horse race actually started in the Isle of Man. So it was a pretty swish upmarket place to stay at plus it was where the Norton team always had their headquarters. I have memories of Gilbert Smith, who was the managing director of Norton, Joe Craig, who was their technical guru. People like Artie Bell, Geoff Duke, Stanley Woods, Jimmy Simpson, Jimmy Guthrie, Walter Rusk, Tim Hunt, all the great, great racing names and they were like uncles to me. Uncle Tim, Uncle Jim, Uncle Stanley. Stanley Woods certainly has to be one of the greatest of all time. People don't know much about Stanley now as he raced before the war yet he won 10 TT races at a time when there were just three races in the week. The 250 on the Monday, 350 on the Wednesday, 500 on the Friday, and that was a fantastic achievement. When I started getting really into it, becoming more involved and getting to know the riders along with the history and the traditions and all that sort of thing, I remember thinking

"10 TT wins, that is incredible, that will never ever be beaten. Nobody, nobody can ever beat 10 TTs",

and of course, now they have. Stanley was a voluble chap and great friends with my father and mother. He had a toffee factory and every year he used to bring me a four pound tin of Stanley Woods TT toffees which lasted me a long time. They were very good too. He was a lovely man. I used to get up at four o'clock in the morning with my dad and we would go up to the Grandstand. In those days, as soon as the sun came over the horizon, they'd be blasting off down Bray Hill. Then you'd get in a car and go around to find somewhere to watch. One of the great things about the Isle of Man is that if you know the roads on the outside and the inside, you can get around and watch from all sorts of places. I was always with people that did know the roads so I could see everything and I saw some absolutely fantastic races over the years. During the practice period, when they came in we would always go to the Cadbury's cocoa tent. It wasn't chocolate, it was Cadbury's cocoa in those days and for a growing child who was now totally absorbed with the TT, you'd be standing with your idols like Jimmy Simpson and Jimmy Guthrie and Tim Hunt and Stanley Woods plus my father, Ernie Nott, Tyrell Smith, people like that. Listening to them it was like watching fishermen in conversation

"a fish this length got away from me"

but it was the TT.

"I just tried to take Hillberry in third gear,I just couldn't quite get around"

For me, this was a wonderful experience.

The Castle Mona was a great social centre. It had a long, long corridor lounge with leather armchairs. I remember the name of the manager was Miss Reese and she was a bit of a dragon, attempting to rule the place with a rod of iron. One particular memory I have is of Derek Mansell, who is sadly now dead, otherwise I wouldn't be telling you this story. He was the son of Bill Mansell and they were both directors of Norton Motors. Bill was the MD. Now, Derek had the next room to me in the Castle Mona hotel and this was in the days when the bedroom door had a fan light over it, which, when opened, provided some pretty crude air conditioning. The fan light in Derek's room was open and the fan light in my room was open. I don't know how old I was. I was pretty young but I went down to breakfast with my mother in the Castle Mona and there's the big ballroom there which was also the dining room with the chandeliers and everything. The riders were there in their leathers because they used to come down to breakfast, ready to go straight up to the Grandstand once they'd eaten. All of a sudden I piped up and said,

"Mummy, I think Uncle Derek is very mean."

"Oh, yeah? Eat your cornflakes dear!" she replied.

My mother knew there was something coming but kids can be very persistent. I said again,

"I think our Uncle Derek's very mean."

"Oh, all right dear, Why?" was her response this time.

"I heard a woman in his room saying if he didn't give her five pounds, she was going to go."

I didn't know what the hell it was that had been going on but everyone on the nearby tables were laughing with the exception of Derek Mansell, a director of Norton Motors. I have so many great memories like that.

Freddie Dixon, who was one of the great riders, won the sidecar TT in 1923. I've got the piston from my father's Norton, which finished in second position in that race. I've kept it on a shelf in my study. Freddie was a bit of a joker. He rode into the ballroom of the Castle Mona one year during dinner on the back of a donkey and he had a stick in front of it with a carrot on the end; things like that were going on in the island all the time. I know that it's all a lot more serious these days. They used to do the most dreadful things. One of the tricks they used to get up to was about three or four of them would get on each end of the horse tram which ran along the seafront on Douglas promenade. Now the horse tram when you look at it, it's got a very short wheelbase, but very long overhang at both ends. The people would jump by numbers. The folks at the front row would jump then those on the back would until this whole thing came off the tracks. Very funny we thought but in retrospect, I wonder what the poor horse would have felt because it must have been terrifying for them. Anyway, they were great times and I never hesitate to say this, the Isle of Man TT is the greatest motor sport event of any kind in my opinion. Nowhere now has the tradition of the TT. No other motorsport event started as early as 1907 and has been held every year with the exception of war years since. No other current event has a circuit, like the Isle of Man, 37 and three quarter miles on public roads. They've improved them year by year and they are still absolutely awesome. The thought of circulating the Isle of Man, even now at an average speed of 125 miles an hour is quite incredible to me.

If Stanley Woods is the most outstanding legendary rider from before the war then Jimmy Guthrie must run him pretty close. He was the first man to do a 60 mile an hour lap, a 70 mile an hour lap and an 80 mile an hour lap in the Isle of Man although he never had the success that Guthrie and Woods had. Stanley wasn't just a brilliant rider, he was a brilliant showman as well. You don't very often get the two things together. Stanley really was absolutely marvellous. I think it was 1935 when he was having a terrific battle, riding a Guzzi. It was something very unusual before the war for a foreign bike to do well. They hardly ever did well with a foreign rider because it took so long for them to learn the TT course. George Meier won on the BMW in 1939 but the first major success for a foreign bike that I remember was the Senior TT in 1935 and Stanley was having this colossal battle with Jimmy Guthrie. They held out a petrol can for him when he was coming out of Governors Bridge down the Glencrutchery Road before disappearing in the distance to indicate that he should come in to refuel at the end of the lap he just started. Jimmy Guthrie was in the lead. Norton had a signalling station at Stella Maris in Ramsey and they phoned through and said in effect

"Okay Jimmy, you roll it back a bit, because Stanley is going to be stopping at the end of the lap he is on now."

So they gave him an appropriate signal at Stella Maris, but it was a dummy. He wasn't gonna stop at all and he didn't. As a result of Jimmy slowing down and Stanley not stopping and speeding up, he won by, I think, four seconds. That was incredible. There was also a chap called Omobono Tenni. We used to call him *'trombone, oh, Tony'*. An Italian, he rode for Moto Guzzi and he was a brilliant rider but the problem for any continental coming over to the TT was that they were riding against people who had been doing it for years. The Brits would go to the TT course and look at it in their own time but it took a continental racer some time in those days. You don't get them now unfortunately at the top level. So it took the continentals three or four years in those days to learn the TT but Tenni was one of the great riders who should have done well. In later years Giacomo Agostini and Carlo Ubialli would prove themselves. Ago was brilliant in the way he quickly got to grips with the TT.

Always in any sport, there is going to be a person or a few people who can do it better than the rest. By virtue of the fact they have better reflexes, better eyesight, more experience. Just a greater ability. I find it very difficult to answer a question of why Woods and Guthrie stood out; they were on the best bikes of course. Jimmy Guthrie was a works Norton rider. Stanley Woods was a works Velocette rider and a works Norton rider and a works Guzzi rider. He was a works Husqvarna rider as well although he never rode it at the TT as far as I know. To be the best it had to be a combination of physical characteristics, determination, experience, skill, having the right bike. Usually there's only one or two people who've got that combination of characteristics and they were two of them. Two very different people. Incidentally, Jimmy Guthrie was very quiet, introverted, and serious. Very nice. Don't misunderstand me, he was a very nice chap. Withdrawn is the word I would use about him plus I would add to that, serious. Stanley Woods meanwhile was bubbly, extrovert, light hearted, jokey, always joshing around with people, enormous fun, great company to be with plus he had the Irish gift of the gab. He could have talked for Ireland.

No Limit was the big film of the time. I was very aware of George Formby, of course, as we all were in those days, because he was one of the top artists. No Limit was and still is, a legend in its own lifetime. A quite incredible film. The old zero to hero story. Everybody took it with a pinch of salt and laughed at it because it couldn't possibly have happened, of course, and he was on this quite dreadful machine with the pseudo-chequered streamlining on it. However, as it was George Formby and because it was the Isle of Man and because it was the TT we were all very flattered. It was regarded as great fun and it became almost mandatory to go and see it as part of your Isle of Man trip. When I went back to the Isle of Man many years later they were showing No Limit then at the Crescent cinema, I think. There is a favourite bit I can dimly recall. It's been a long time since I've seen it but I seem to remember that for some reason he went into the pub at Ballacraine to have a drink and Ballacraine was where I did my first ever TT commentary in 1949. I had done my first ever commentary for the BBC on the British Grand Prix. It wasn't the Formula One Grand Prix in those days because Formula One didn't start until 1950. I'd done my first commentary on the British Grand Prix at Silverstone in 1949 and then the BBC said to me,

"Look, can you help out on the motorcycle thing? We've got the TT and the Isle of Man, perhaps it isn't your scene."

I thought

"Oh, wow. Fantastic! It was very much my scene."

So I went to the Isle of Man, for the BBC. My commentary position was at Ballacraine. I didn't have a commentary box. I was festooned in wires and I had a sort of harness thing where the lip mic stuck in the front of it. So I just put my head forward and talked because I needed both hands free to handle my clipboard with information and stopwatches, all that sort of thing. I vividly remember Les Graham on the 7R works AJS barrelling down the road towards me from the direction of Douglas and he was going far too fast. He overshot. I thought he was going to take the corner because I didn't know how quickly you could go around it yet he damn near disembowelled me with his clutch lever. He stopped successfully and disappeared up the road. So Ballacraine, No Limit, George Formby, Murray Walker, BBC, they all sort of roll up into one big memory for me.

The TT of 1949 was the very first round of the brand new World Motorcycle Championship, which I remember primarily because of the Ballacraine incident in the Junior TT. He was riding the fabled AJS Porcupine in the Senior race and he broke down so failed to win but unless I'm very much mistaken, that was the year that Harold Daniel won on the Norton. Now, on top of the incredible people that rode for Norton, because if you'd seen Harold Daniel out of his leathers, away from the Isle of Man and the TT and you said to somebody, that man has won the

Senior TT, you would have been invited to go and get your head examined. He was rotund, bald-ish and wore round granny glasses; looked as If he couldn't even start a motorcycle, nevermind ride one. Yet he was absolutely brilliant. It was Harold Daniel that invented the phrase featherbed to describe the works Norton. I know how all that happened. I spent a lot of my childhood in Ireland, in Belfast, around there and became very involved with the motorcycle scene. One of my great friends was Artie Bell who subsequently became a Norton works rider. They had a very healthy, thriving motorcycle grass track scene in Northern Ireland, as well as the road racing on these incredible circuits that only the Irish would ride on such as the Northwest 200, at Portrush. There was a guy called Cromie McCandless who rode on grass tracks, and his brother Rex was a brilliantly gifted, self taught engineer. He was a bit of a headcase in many ways and I mean that in the nicest way because he was also an inspiring bloke. Now Rex had built for Artie, a special Triumph with a twin-cylinder engine and a spring frame. The back wheel was on a lever and there was a spring between the lever and what we know now is a spring frame. So Rex McCandless built this thing, and Cromie was winning everything. At that time, the works Norton was what we used to call the old garden gate with plunger springing at the back, which they really needn't have bothered with because it didn't move very much. It did have telescopic forks on the front. Artie Bell, knowing about Cromie and Rex McCandless was consistently getting at Gilbert Smith, the managing director of Norton, and Joe Craigy, the technical director to go and look at this bike yet they initially took no notice. He finally persuaded them to go and have a look. He rode a Manx Norton at Bangor against Cromie McCandless on his Triumph with its spring frame and Cromie won in front of Gilbert Smith and Joe Craig who especially was very impressed. They commissioned Rex McCandless to produce a new frame and that was the featherbed Norton, which became legendary, and rightly so. In my opinion, it's probably the greatest racing motorcycle that has ever been produced, taking into account all the races that it won and the period of time that it did them in. When Harold Daniel rode this for the first time, after being used to the old garden gate thing, this was in 1950 he said, 'it's like riding a feather bed'. That's when it became called the featherbed Norton. The next year, of course, was the year that Geoff Duke won the 1951 TT. Your heroes in life, I think, are created to some extent, according to the time that they were riding or driving and the time that you were watching them. I think in 1950, I was at my most impressionable. The TT was heaven to me. They were all heroes. I knew Geoff, because I was working in Birmingham for Dunlop and at that time, Geoff, having won the Senior Manx Grand Prix on the Norton in 1949 was obviously a bloke to watch and then in 1950 he rode on one when he appears with this one piece, glove leather suit, when all the others were riding these great old suits. Jack Brett, I remember, had shoulders on him like a barn door and it was mostly padding. Geoff Duke applied himself to it and he'd got Frank Barker who was a friend of his at St. Helens and made gloves to make him a one piece suit out of very thin leather. So his wind resistance was cut down. Geoff was literally God-like walking along in this leather suit. When he push-started the bike he just dropped onto it. It was as though they'd been moulded together as he disappeared down Bray Hill. That I remember as one of the greatest races of all time.

In 1955, my father was still alive and he was the BBC's lead commentator at the TT Grandstand. There were several other commentators dotted around the 37 and three quarter miles and as far as I remember, I was at Creg Ny Baa. So I wasn't able to be aware of everything that was happening around the course unlike my father who had a producer with him who decided to go to this or that place. In those days, the riders weren't seeded as they are now where you get the best ones at the front. Back then Geoff Duke won one year when he was number 57. So you could have anybody from number 1 to number 57, potentially able to win the TT. Geoff, by now, was on the Gilera and this was a marriage made in heaven. He'd left Norton and had gone to Gilera; he'd been a lone, single British rider on the single-cylinder Norton, which was a totally outclassed bike, competing against the MV four-cylinders, the Guzzi twins and the Gileras. At that time the TT was so important in motorcycle racing, it was more important than all the rest of the races put together. To win the TT was every constructor's ambition and certainly Gilera wanted to win the TT yet they hadn't succeeded in doing so. So they got Geoff Duke to ride for them who was the supreme talent of the day and now on the supreme bike of the day. Reggie Armstrong from Ireland was his teammate. I can remember actually walking through the paddock, the weigh-in, behind the Gilera mechanics pushing Geoff Duke's Gilera. It's the silly things you do in life that can mean so much therefore I touched the mud guard of the Gilera. I just wanted to touch it. I thought that's the bike that could win. Well, Geoff, rode absolutely brilliantly. I listened on the headphones to my father waxing lyrically about the fact that it had finally happened. It's happened at last, the first 100 mile an hour lap at the TT and Geoff Duke has done it on the Gilera.

I remember being very, very excited because Geoff was and still is a friend of mine. I felt that he was getting the just reward from having made the move from Norton to Gilera, which he'd delayed for a long time. I mean, Geoff Duke riding against people like Umberto Masetti on the continent where he was giving away miles an hour and still beating them. So I thought, at last, the 100 mph had been broken but then sadly we got the news that it wasn't 100 miles an hour. It was, if I remember correctly, 99.97 miles an hour. And I... do... not... believe... that in the days when they were doing the timekeeping on the old turnip stop watches, that they could actually have been as accurate as that. Maybe just maybe, Geoff was actually cheated out of the 100 mile an hour lap. It wasn't until two years later when Bob McIntyre did it on the Gilera, that it stuck.

1957 was as far as I can remember the only time we've ever had an eight lap TT. What a feat of endurance, stamina, determination, skill, ability, and everything else that's required of a top rider to do eight laps around the TT. Absolutely fantastic. Bob McIntyre sadly is not known to today's enthusiasts because he was killed a long time ago in 1962 at Oulton Park. He was a really lovely man, a quiet, friendly, cheerful Scotsman.

"1957 was as far as I can remember the only time we've ever had an eight lap TT. What a feat of endurance, stamina, determination, skill, ability, and everything else that's required of a top rider to do eight laps around the TT."

MURRAY WALKER

He had a fantastic physique plus enormous ability and until he rode the Gilera he was like Geoff, he never really got a bike that was worthy of his talents. Then he rode the Honda but in the lesser classes. That hundred mile an hour lap of his was incredible, not as incredible as Geoff Duke's, in my opinion, because after all, Geoff had done it two years earlier, to within a fraction of a second, but just to underline his class, Bob McIntyre didn't do one 100 mile an hour lap, he did several 100 mile an hour laps. I was at Creg ny Baa that year and one of my abiding memories is seeing Bob McIntyre on the Gilera, catching John Surtees on the MV who was another legendary TT personality. Bob had started behind John Surtees and was just behind him as they came around Kate's cottage, down the approach to the Creg, to the turn right and then on toward Brandish. McIntyre was closing up on Surtees and I remember saying, just listen to this and they were changing gear at different times because Surtees was in front and McIntyre was behind. So you've got this fantastic MV-4 changing, Gilera-4 changing, MV-4 changing, Gilera-4 changing and I've never heard anything like it before or since.

Honda arrived to compete in 1959. I'm willing to be corrected on the date, but they actually came to the Isle of Man in any form, first in 1954. When this small party of Japanese people came over, and they were not flavour of the year, nevermind flavour of the month because in 1954 it was just eight years or so after the end of the war, and that's not a very long time. We'd had these dreadful atrocities from the Japanese, against our troops during the war and this was the first appearance they made, plus it was the first time any of us had ever seen a Japanese person. So they came over with a bit of a cloud hanging over them. There were some and I think I must have been one of them, who thought well, you know, the war's over now so turn the other cheek and all that stuff. Yet you would go up to these people and adopt the time honoured British procedure of speaking to foreigners, slowly and loud. You would say

"where are you from, where are you from"?

"Honda Motor Company"

"What?"

"Honda Motor Company"

"Honda?"

"Honda Motor Company"

"Ah, Honda Motor Company, what do you do?"

"We make motorcycles."

"Oh, you make motorcycles? Why are you here?"

"Next year, we come, TT races"

"Oh, next year TT races. Will it be the Kamikaze special? Who will ride for you? Harry Kari? Will he ride?"

We all thought this was very funny, these anti-Japanese jokes. They then disappeared. They didn't come back the next year, in 1955, as they said they were going to. Mr. Honda was one of those people. Soichiro Honda, the great man who started this fantastic company, which now has won over 500 Motorcycle Grand Prix, been at the top of Formula One, production cars, motor boats, aeroplanes, you name it. All this has happened in my time. So one of these men was Mr. Honda himself and he realised that he had bitten off more than he could chew in wanting to come back next year. But they did come back in 1959. Now when they had been over in 1954 they had been taking photographs of the Norton, the works Norton in particular. The engine, the petrol tanks, the rear suspension, the front suspension, the carburetor, you name it, anything. They said they were coming back to race in the 125 class. We thought the Japanese had a reputation in those days of being very good copyists so we believed they're going to be back with a Manx Norton with a 125cc hole in the barrel. When they came back in 1959 with the 125cc bikes, they were 4-valve, double overhead camshaft, twin-cylinder, spring frame, telescopic forked devices that were light years ahead of anything that we had in that class. They had an American, Major Bill Hunt, who was in charge of the team. I can't remember all the riders but one I do was Kunimitsu Takahashi. They didn't win the race but they won the team prize. Now for a manufacturer from Japan with a brand new bike, never having been to the TT before to come over with three Japanese riders and win the team prize was a fantastic achievement which showed how ignorant we were about the whole thing. When Mr. Honda first came over in 1954 he actually went to the Isle of Wight first, in the belief that that was where the TT was held. He got it right in the end. My goodness, he got it right in the end when you look at what Honda have achieved since then, absolutely incredible.

Something that people forget or maybe people don't realise is that Mike Hailwood won not only three TTS in 1961 but he darn nearly won four TTs that year because he was riding an AJS in the 350 and leading when he broke down near Milltown cottage. I think it was there, I'm not absolutely sure but it was in that area. To win three TTs in a week is incredible. Four, which he came within an ace of doing in the same week would have been, well, nigh unbelievable but it was a mark of the genius and I use the word advisedly. For me, Mike Hailwood is the greatest racing motorcyclist who has ever lived. Now that point of view is conditioned by my age and the fact that he was a personal friend of mine plus I've stayed with him at his home and all the rest of it. Yes, there's been a lot of very great motorcycle riders but there haven't been any, in my opinion, with the combination of ability and charisma, laid back attitude, fun and sheer brilliance of Mike Hailwood. He was made to ride a motorcycle. It just came instinctively to him; he didn't have to work at it. It was because of Stan Hailwood, Mike's father that really made Mike because Stan was a gigantically successful businessman and a multimillionaire in the days when a million pounds was a lot more than it is now. Stan had started his career, his business career, selling ties from an attache case to draper's in Manchester; he was walking around the streets, a natural born salesman. Then he got into the motorcycle business and he developed Kings of Oxford, which was the leading chain of motorcycle dealers. They made an enormous amount of money. He raced motorcycles himself, but he had a problem with his foot so he wore a boot with a big thick soul on it. Stan walked in a very ungainly way. He used to race a Norton sidecar outfit, fairly successfully, but he could never do what he wanted to do, which was ride a solo bike. When Mike was born, and then grew up, he went to the Naval College at Pangbourne. One of Stan Hailwood's characteristics was that he almost invariably fell out with anybody he had anything to do with. He fell out with the Admiral who ran the Naval Academy at Pangbourne so took Mike away and put him into the Kings of Oxford business. Mike started riding and in 1957 Stan got his friend Bill Webster to lend Mike a 125cc MV to race at Oulton Park and I was there to commentate on this. Mike didn't win but he did well and Stan realised he had got a one-off on his hands. Stan being Stan could see Mike as something that he wanted to be himself. He could see Mike as an invaluable publicity medium for the Kings of Oxford business. He also saw him as increasing his personal status so he poured money into him. Literally. He got Ducati to make special bikes just for Mike. One of the leading tuners of the day was a chap called Bill Lacey. He came in the same bracket as Steve Lancefield and Francis Beer who both did a lot of tuning for the team riders at the TT, so Stan Hailwood employed Bill Lacy full time to work on Mike's bikes. For two reasons. One, he was one of the best you could get, and two, if he employed him full-time, no one else would be able to use typical Stan thinking.

He then sent Mike off to South Africa with Dave Chadwick for a season's racing to give him more experience and from there Mike took off, he came back and won the British championship. He then won every British Works Championship and started riding in the TT. Honda employed him and what an incredible period that was on the 125, 250-4,350-6, and 500 cc bikes. It was a series of fantastic races against riders like Derek Minter, Bob McIntyre, Jim Redman, Ralph Bryans, Stuart Graham, a flood of names come to mind and Mike beat them all.

Mike's first TT must have been around about 1958 while Geoff Duke was on the BMW. Geoff rode one more year on the Norton so it was the tail end of Geoff's career and the beginning of Mike's, so you couldn't fairly compare them. It's certainly true to say that as Geoff's star waned, Mike's career started, so the British had two superheroes to worship, which sadly, they haven't gotten now.

I've got so many memories that they tend to crowd each other out and I remember '65 and Agostini arriving. What a gigantic impact he had. He and Mike had a lot of things in common. They were both very friendly. They could both pull any girl that ever went to the Isle of Man. And probably did so! They were great friends. They were both the sons of millionaires. They were both inspired riders and if you had written the script for the British Grand Prix in 1967 for a film, it would have been rejected as being too fanciful. You had this incredible situation of Mike Hailwood in his last year because it was his final one for Honda and you had Agostini who had won the previous year. They were like two peas in a pod in some ways and totally different in others. You had the Mercurial Latin in Agostini, a very good looking, very personable bloke and you had the laid back archetype Brit in Mike Hailwood. They came together for the TT in 1967 which was the Diamond Jubilee year and possibly the greatest TT of all time, Hailwood against Agostini. Ago was riding the MV-3 cylinder, which ironically, had been developed by Mike Hailwood, the year before Mike had moved to Honda.

So Agostini was on a brilliant bike, developed by his arch-rival, and the Italian, unlike a lot of continental riders, had mastered the TT circuit and had done so incredibly quickly. He's up against Mike Hailwood, in my opinion, the greatest rider who ever lived. Certainly the greatest TT rider that has ever lived. He was on the 4-cylinder 500 Honda and the Japanese manufacturer's attitude at that time was more power, they always wanted more power, the word handling was not considered so much and in comparison with the 3-cylinder MV, which had virtually ideal characteristics for the TT in terms of power, power delivery and handling. Don't forget it was developed by Mike. The Honda had gigantic power but handled like a five bar gate. Now, I can't remember all the nuances of the '67 Senior race but the point is that Mike and Agostini were battling each other, you could forget about anybody else in the race. You've got this big crowd watching because of this battle that was gonna be happening, and because it was the Diamond Jubilee TT and so on. Everyone was absolutely on tenterhooks with the lead changing, not just lap by lap but place by place. Mike Hailwood came into the pits with a time deficiency, he'd been 10 seconds down, then a few seconds ahead, then 10 seconds down again. As Agostini regained the time, they came into the pits virtually together. Mike had a loose twist grip, I mean, as if having too much power and not enough handling wasn't a big enough problem, he'd actually got a loose twist grip. Now, those people who ride motorcycles will know that having a loose twist grip, and I've had one in trials and motocross and things, you don't know how to handle it because you don't know how much power is coming but just as Mike Hailwood won a TT on the MV after he'd fallen off in the wet and broken the windscreen he seemed to be able to overcome all these things. Now he had this loose twistgrip. He came into the pit and said,

'Give me a hammer.'

Mike's ability as a mechanic was about as great as my ability with electronics; he was absolutely useless. He stood there hammering away at the end of the handlebar, quite what he thought he was going to achieve I do not know but he got away and of course Agostini was back in the lead again, as he'd got out before Mike Hailwood. Sadly we never got the climax to the race that we would ideally have achieved with both of them finishing and who is going to come out on top? I can imagine my father getting absolutely frenetic in the Grandstand talking about waiting for the light to come on at Governor's bridge over the riders number on the scoreboard to show they were at Governor's Bridge because Agostini broke a chain at Windy Corner or somewhere around there. Allegedly, he coasted and pushed in. What he did is quite amazing and not only amazing but an indication of what sort of a bloke Agostini is because most riders would have said 'the hell with it' and just sat there and waited for the recovery vehicle to come. It was a fantastic race.

In 1975, Mick Grant broke Mike Hailwood's lap record and I think maybe it just goes to show how fantastic Mike was because he held it for eight years before it was broken.

I don't wish to take anything away from Mick because he was riding the Kawasaki which, just as the 500 cc Honda had not been an ideal motorcycle for the TT nor was the 2-stroke Kawasaki an ideal bike for the TT. Mick Grant actually still has that bike; he brought it to the TT riders Riders Association dinner one year. That was a hell of an achievement by Mick to break Mike's record but when you consider how much earlier that record had been created, it just shows how good Mike Hailwood was.

Somebody who gets overlooked in the history of the TT for some reason, I can't possibly fathom why, is John Surtees. Absolutely fantastic rider, multiple TT winner, multiple World Champion, the only person who's ever gone on as a motorcycle World Champion to become Formula One World Champion, which he did in 1964. John had a brilliant career briefly as a Norton rider in the TT but of course, he made his name with MV. In those years, he won repeatedly and I've always felt it was terribly unfair that people say, '*Oh, yeah, but John Surtees won on the MV because there wasn't any opposition*'. Gilera had withdrawn and the MV-4 was infinitely better than anything he was against, that is perfectly true but just as people used to say about Mike Hailwood, the only reason he's winning is because his dad is spending a lot of money on him. I would say about John Surtees that, once you put your leg across the bike, it's down to you. John won the races, he not only won them but did so at record speeds. Many overlook the fact that in 1957, John was on the MV up against the Gilera which was a better bike, he was up against the Guzzi V8, he was up against the BMW, he was up against the Norton's, he was up against the Matchless machines. 1957 is a magical year for the TT because it was during that year that you've got this mass withdrawal. Gilera pulled out, MV stayed on but John actually spent a lot of his career riding against top people on top bikes, and he's never, in my opinion, been given due credit for it.

Meanwhile, Mike Hailwood went away to New Zealand to start a new life and to be honest, I don't know what the motivation was for him to come back to compete in the Isle of Man, who put him up to it or how difficult it was to persuade him especially considering how long he'd been out and considering how much he had to lose. It was an incredible thing to do because there he was, with this unblemished shining reputation as the great multiple World Champion, multiple TT winner Mike Hailwood, years later, putting himself on the line against the then top people and returning to the scene of so many triumphs, to ride the Ducati, a bike he'd never ridden. To win as he did was fairytale stuff and he did it so brilliantly, so easily. Just another indication of what a fantastic person he was. Then, as if that wasn't enough, he'd now got the taste for it so he came back the following year, and won the Senior TT, on the Suzuki, another new bike to him. I can never find words strong enough to express my admiration and respect for Mike.

I have a gigantic respect for Graham Crosby and people like him. When I say people like him I mean, Harry Hinton who is a name that most people have never heard of. He was an Australian who came over like Tony MacAlpine, a Sydney taxi driver who rode a Gilera Saturno in the Senior TT and these people have come literally from the other side of the world because the Isle of Man TT is the holy grail. It isn't so much now but it was then the holy grail for anybody who had any desire to do well in motorcycle racing. You had the colonials as we then called them coming over and to a man, they were very good. They had to be good to raise the money to get here. People like Hinton were superb tuners of bikes and they could make their self-built Manx Norton's go faster than the works ones. Graham Crosby had come all the way from New Zealand. Somebody that we didn't know from a bar of soap, brilliant rider, great personality, real credit to the sport. I was with him very recently, actually and I hadn't seen him for years and years yet he had not changed at all. He is still great fun as he was then. I wish we'd got more of them now.

I don't know if it's just time lending a certain amount of charm to my memories but around then, before the war, the weather always seemed to be brilliant for the TT. It was always hot and sunny plus the tar on the course was forever melting. Obviously, they didn't have the tyre compounds then that they have now but one of the problems used to be melting tar and the loss of grip you could have as a result of it. The prize giving at the Villa Marina gardens was a magical affair because the public were also present; it wasn't just the Cognoscenti and the elite that were there. The public were present, sitting in these sort of folding wooden deck chairs. The ceremony was done in the evening and the riders would appear, the posh ones in suits and collars with ties, people like Artie Bell and not so posh ones wearing just trousers and the neck shirt. They were all wonderfully received because the enthusiast had his idols in front of him. The winner would always be literally chaired from the back of the crowd, right through everyone, put on the stage and get up on stage to receive that wonderful, wonderful Mercury statue. I've got 15 replicas which my father won and the Senior TT, the enormous one, of course was the one to have. So to be at the Villa Marina, as I was many, many, many times with the big shots, and in this euphoric atmosphere was an incredible experience.

Mad Sunday before the war, if it happened, it would have happened to a much lesser extent than today, simply because of the fact that people didn't have as many vehicles in those days. Yes, there were a lot of motorcycles but there weren't as many as there are now I'd suspect. I used to take part in Mad Sunday. I used to get my bike and go blasting around with them. I used to be able to recite all the milestones, I can still do a lot of them. I used to be able to recite all the milestones of the TT and the way I learned was by going around on the bike. I had a BMW. I used to go wafting around on that. Of course, you've got some complete and utter maniacs. What you didn't get then that I understand you get now is an enormous number of continental tourists, and in particular Germans, who don't actually know which way round to go or didn't in those days. I think it was 1936 when the top German rider was a bloke called Karl Gall. He actually started and I can't imagine how it happened with all the discipline, but he actually started one of the practice periods blasting off in the wrong direction. He left the Glencrutchery road and whizzed off towards Governor's bridge.

When I used to take friends around the Isle of Man in the car. I used to sort of have a macabre tour, where I would say in Union Mills, there is a post office and Freddy Hicks actually hit the post box in the wall and killed himself. Then I'd say this is Birkin's corner where Birkin was killed.

This is Handley's corner wall, he wasn't killed but that's where he fell off. This is Doran's bend and so on. If you know the history of TT, you can literally go around and identify places where somebody did something.

There is quite simply nothing like the Isle of Man TT anywhere in the world nor will there ever be.

Murray passed away on March 13th, 2021 aged 97 years of age. Like the Isle of Man TT he was a completely unique character and his love for the event was evident on the many occasions he returned to the Island in his later years.

BARRY WOOD

Born Douglas, Isle of Man

TT Years 1998, 2000-2006
1 x 17th, 1 x 19th, 1 x 23rd, 1 x 24th, 1 x 25th, 1 x 28th, 1 x 31st, 1 x 32nd, 1 x35th, 1 x40th, 3 x DNF

MGP Years 1988-1992, 1994, 1996-2003, 2005-06
2 x 1st, 4 x 2nd, 3 x 3rd, 1 x 4th, 1 x 5th, 1 x 6th, 3 x 7th, 1 x 15th, 1 x 17th, 1 x 22nd, 1 x 25th, 1 x 28th, 6 x DNF

For every Dunlop, Hislop and McGuinness TT success story there are many other riders who fill the oversubscribed grid on the Glencrutchery Road every year, each with no hope of getting anywhere near the podium yet still take on the most famous circuit in the world. Anyone who has watched the bikes leave the start line will know it takes almost a quarter of an hour for all the bikes to go on their way and no sooner is the last one away it's only a few short minutes before the leaders come around to begin their second lap. That's how big the grid is. Barry Wood is one such racer, a local lad with the TT running through his veins plus a real passion for the Manx Grand Prix. While the star names would be preparing for the Isle of Man by racing at British championship week in, week out he, like the majority of riders during his era, would hold everyday jobs and spend every spare penny they had just to race the Isle of Man. Barry may never have rubbed elbows with the 'greats' but as a TT racer he has a great tale to tell.

I was two days old when I attended my first motorcycle road race. That's right. Not two years or two months or even two weeks but two days old. I have my Mum to thank for that. As a young girl, Barbara Bell lived where the National Sports Centre in Douglas is now, which is quite close to Quarterbridge. Then it was Millmount cottages on the river bank at Old Spring Valley. Their next door neighbour was Barbara Gibb who had two little boys called Barry and Maurice. They went on to become the Bee Gees and even when they rose to fame and she'd moved to the United States, the pair continued their friendship, keeping in touch right into their later years. My mum was born in 1941 and her father, my Grandad, was serving in the Second World War. When he used to come home on leave he would say

"*It won't be long now until we can go and watch the motorbikes coming down the road.*"

She didn't understand what he meant but as soon as wartime was over she was taken by the hand to Quarterbridge to watch the Manx Grand Prix in 1946. This was the first resumption of racing on the Mountain course with the TT returning the following summer. So my Grandad had kept his promise. He was a Scout master when the scoreboards were first introduced on Glencrutchery Road in 1922 so he would have been in charge of the boys as they posted up the hand painted times of the riders. Like his Dad, he would sometimes take my Mum to watch, often at Braddan Bridge until they moved to Willaston, which is near the Grandstand, in 1951. She was at the bottom of Bray Hill for the Senior TT in 1953 and saw Les Graham's fatal accident which upset her greatly.

Mum met and married my Dad, then towards the end of 1962 she found herself expecting me, her first child. Heavily pregnant she managed to watch the TT in 1963 albeit in discomfort. She was working at Woolworths in Strand Street at that time yet saw all the races as they would let her go to watch as long as she went back to work in the evenings. Come the Manx Grand Prix she missed all of practice week waiting for me to arrive. I turned up at the Jane Crookall maternity home in Douglas on the Saturday night after the final practice. On the Monday she packed everything up, ready to go with me in the pram until the matron arrived and ordered her to get back into bed. A blazing row ensued.

"*Mrs Wood, you have responsibilities now towards your child.*"

"*Bugger the baby,*" my Mum replied. *"I've missed all of Grand Prix practice week. There's a race on Tuesday, I'll be there to watch and so will he."* At that time it was just the Junior and Senior races at the Manx on Tuesday and Thursday respectively. So at two days old I was up at Governor's Bridge in the pram for the Junior Manx Grand Prix. I had no chance of not becoming involved really!

Back in those days, many local people went to watch the TT and the Manx Grand Prix. Around 30 or so years ago I was at my Nan's house compiling a racing quiz. She was watching Crossroads and when that was on you weren't allowed to speak or make any kind of noise. I turned to my Mum and asked if it was okay to quietly run through some questions with her.

"*Ssh, ssh, ssh,*" retorted my Nan. So even more quietly I said to my Mum.

"Name the rider back in the 1920s who was known as The Wasp because of the black and yellow striped jumper he wore when riding?"

Without taking her eyes off the screen my Nan said,

"Ohhh Tommy Spann. He was a good rider."

Which shows what kind of an impact the racing had on those living in the Isle of Man during those times.

When I was four, maybe five I was taken to watch the practices but I'd end up bawling my eyes out because of the noise. I remember seeing Phil Read and Bill Ivy lining up for the 125cc race in 1968. This was the year when they both dominated the smaller bike categories with Yamaha ordering them to win a world title each, Ivy the 250 and Read the 125 but having wrapped up his championship Read is said to have ignored team orders and took what should have been his team-mate's crown as well. Ivy's consolation was recording the first 100mph lap on a 125 and I was there to see it. I watched the start in what was known as the Donkey

Field, right in behind the timekeeper's box, standing directly behind the starter who was holding his flag on his little podium. I could see the riders' whites of their eyes through their goggles from my position standing on the wall. I thought it was great until it became too noisy with lots of little silver coloured bikes and their orange or yellow stripes so I was taken to my Nan's house which was a ten minute walk away in the nearby Willaston estate. My Mum then ran back to watch the Senior.

By 1970 I was begging to be allowed to watch the practices and races so I think my Mum was secretly glad that she had an ally, albeit one of such a young age. My Dad wasn't interested. He was a horse racing man. So all the way through to my teenage years it was inevitable that I would have a motorbike on my 16th birthday. It was no surprise that I eventually started racing and it was absolutely no surprise that one day I would race the roads, the Manx GP and the TT. That was how I was brought up.

My first taste of TT fame, if you could call it that, was in 1971 when the Daily Express ran a competition to name the greatest rider of all time. They'd printed a list which included Mike Hailwood, Giacomo Agostini, Stanley Woods, Geoff Duke, Bob McIntyre and other similar great TT riders. You had to pick your top three and then, as was always the case, fill in a tie-breaker. So with the help of my Mum I picked my favourite trio with Hailwood in top spot; we sent it off and thought no more about it. Back in those days the national UK newspapers always covered the TT and quite often gave away stickers with their publications. A couple of nights later, there was a knock at the front door. Very few folk had telephones then. My Mum answered and I could hear this conversation,

"*Yes, yes, Barry is here. Who are you please?*"

It was a reporter from the Daily Express, her name was Lindsey Mackie and she had a photographer with her called Peter Jackson. She explained about the competition and how they were amazed that someone so young should submit an entry, therefore felt I deserved a special prize. So we had a short interview and I posed out in the garden with a Honda-6, not the full size 250 but a scaled down Motomodelli version. My picture was in the following day's newspaper with a report that said *'this seven year old boy would be given a special prize in the coming days'.* Friday's Senior TT was approaching so the Express came to our house the day before and said,

"Look, there's a chance that this race may not go ahead tomorrow. If that's the case, be ready to go."

That is in fact what happened with the Senior pushed back a day. So I was scrubbed from head to toe, best shorts, knee high white socks plus blazer with various motorcycle racing badges on it and taken to the back of the TT Grandstand where the top reporter of the time, Leslie Nichol, was waiting. He shook my hand telling me I was a wonderful young TT supporter. Next it was off to the Palace Hotel on Douglas promenade for my prize. We arrived to be greeted by Lyndsey who said that someone special would be here to meet us shortly. Sure enough, in came none other than World champion Giacomo Agostini. He was wearing his red and black leathers this year having only worn just black in the past plus he also had on his one piece yellow waterproof suit. I was too shy to speak at first. I did get his autograph and had a few little words while the reporters chipped in with questions. That lasted about 10 or 15 minutes until they said he had to go as he's very busy. They took some pictures with one photograph of Ago and myself appearing on the front page of the following day's Express. When I went back to school they stood me in front of the assembly and the headmaster told the kids I had met Agostini which prompted a big round of applause.

Living in Willaston so close to the course you couldn't avoid the TT. As a child I would lie in bed in the morning and be woken by the bikes as they left the Grandstand for early morning practice. Then I would go back to sleep but not for long as you heard them again, coming around Signpost and because back in those days there was no Glen Park estate, no homes either at Governor's Hill, it was just open fields so therefore nothing to block the sounds of the bikes which were a lot noisier back then. I would often ask if I could get up early to go and watch but Mum insisted I was still too young. However in 1972 I sneaked off on my own to watch MGP practice. My Dad was a postman so he was always up early for work. I asked him to wake me early so I could have a cup of tea with him insisting I was usually awake at that time as I heard him when he was pottering about downstairs. So he did and shortly after our cuppa he said he'd better get going as he had to be at the Sorting office which was on the other side of the course. Two minutes after he'd gone I was on my way heading to Greenfield Road. I found a spot on the wall and could see the bikes all lined up under the street lights. This was the first year that the newcomers wore white jackets. Standing in front of me were Phil Haslam with his long hair looking very determined and his sponsor Mal Carter. Suddenly a police sergeant carrying a big stick came over and said

"*You're up very early this morning on your own, young man.*"

I explained about my father going to work early so the copper offered to take me across to the Grandstand to watch from there. I declined but he said if I had any problems I was to give him a wave and he would bring me across the road. Imagine that happening today! After practice had finished I returned home and went back to bed. My Mum was still asleep so therefore none the wiser until Dad came home and told her he'd woken me. She twigged what had happened and asked if I'd gone to the practices to which I confessed I had. Not too much was said but I think she was quite pleased about it. From then on we watched everything together. The Manx Grand Prix was during the school summer holidays so we didn't miss anything. The only one I didn't see was the infamous 125cc TT race in which Gilberto Parlotti was killed on the Mountain. We didn't go because the weather was wild so I listened to it on the wireless at my Nan's as Mum had to work that day.

Once I was old enough to ride on the roads I did so. Unfortunately, I was a bit wild. I was banned for four months for speeding at over a hundred miles an hour on Douglas prom where the limit is only thirty and another time I crashed into some sheep belonging to John Kennaugh, who a lot of people will remember from Radio TT and I'm sorry to say I killed three of them.

It took about a year to get everything sorted out insurance-wise but I was 20 when I began racing. I managed to get what I needed in terms of a licence to tackle the Mountain course but it took me four years. Like many others I had to pay for everything myself when I started so almost every spare penny went in. The rare luxury would be the odd pint or two at my local, the Manor. I'd sometimes have a couple with a guy called Bill Parry who used to be local racer Phil Hogg's boss at the building firm McArd's. We'd often talk about racing over a pint and he'd asked how much the Manx Grand Prix entries were going to cost me. I told him £75 per race and I was entered in two. Next time we met, just as he was leaving to go, he handed me an envelope and said

"*This is to help you*".

Inside was £150 which was very generous but I found it somewhat embarrassing to the point that I stopped going to the pub as I thought how could I go in there and spend money on beer while accepting hand-outs. Nobody had ever given me anything towards racing before. When I eventually went back months later he was there at the bar and said

"*Where the hell have you been?*"

When I explained why he called me a stupid bugger, telling me there's no need to hide from the world. He'd helped me because he wanted to.

So my entry forms for the Manx Grand Prix of 1988 were in. There were five locals. Phil Gilmour, Dave Black, Trevor Burden and Brian Kneale who were also riding in my class. Earlier in the year I'd been to the North West 200 in Northern Ireland and was sitting in the Grand-stand talking to some people from nearby Coleraine when this bloke said

"Do you see that boy over there with his foot in plaster?"

I could see this young guy sitting down with crutches and a broken ankle. He added

"That's McCallen. He is going to be in your race at the Manx. Don't try to stay with him or you'll get hurt."

I thought '*Oh, shit!*

This was when the reality of what I was about to do began to kick in. I'd raced at Cadwell Park, Carnaby, places like that so I was getting to know a few other riders' names. When I looked at the entry list for the Manx there was Darren Powell along with Mark Langton and Steven

Elliott who is still going in the Classic races plus Richard Whiteman. These were all good riders from around the UK, winning several races every weekend so it was exciting to see my name in the programme next to the number 73 that I had been assigned; Philip McCallen was no 76.

This was the first Manx Grand Prix when the opening practice was held on Saturday evening. Prior to that it had always been Monday morning for a long, long time, possibly forever. It was my Mountain course debut and I wanted to be first away. It was something I'd helped other riders do, especially some Irish friends of mine where I've taken their bikes down in the middle of the night and stayed with them until the scrutineering tent opened so they could be first away on the road. I'd helped Donal Hughes, Pat McLaughlin, Seamus Rice, Phil Lunney and I hoped one day I'd get the chance to do that. This time perhaps it was a little easier as this session was in the evening yet I still arrived there early. I was a couple of years away from learning to drive a car so I rode the bike down the short hop from my house to the Grandstand with the stand around my head. I was followed by my Mum who carried a little bag full of spanners, screwdrivers, cable ties, duct tape plus all the other things you needed. That was how sophisticated we were. As we took our place I could see Phil McCallen's big transporter with his name on. A case of the haves and have nots so to speak. I was being helped by another local racer, Tony Duncan, and before the opening session I was violently sick around the back of his car.

"Bloody hell, you're meant to be enjoying yourself," he said to which I replied. *"I know, it's just nerves. I've waited a long time for this day"*.

Back then everyone went out on the course together, unlike today where they're in different classes and newcomers have their own special lap. I was at the front as planned and was beckoned forward by an official holding a piece of paper. She looked at me then looked at the paper just to check that whoever had been through the scrutineering bay was in their rightful place on the road. I suddenly found myself asking

"*What the bloody hell am I doing here*?"

I was shaken from this thought by a '*bam, bam, bam, bam, bam*' noise coming from my right and it was Ian Simpson on a Suzuki Senior bike. He had done the Manx the year before on a TZR so this was his second time. I looked across at him and he gave me a nod. I knew now this was the real thing. I looked behind and it was just a sea of bikes as far as you could see. Then I had the voice in my ear going

"Listen, if you don't want to do it, you don't have to. No-one will think any less of you," while in my other ear it was *"Bugger that, let's just get going."*

Next someone came along with a sign saying STOP ENGINES so it soon went silent and you could hear a pin drop. Suddenly, out of the speakers you hear the voice of the Clerk of the Course, Jackie Wood.

"Good evening everybody. Welcome to the Manx Grand Prix of 1988. Weather conditions are perfect all around the course. Now a word for newcomers. If a faster rider passes you watch what he does. Don't try to stay with him. Just watch what he does and you'll learn from them."

That's how it always was. Then away we went. In the first practice, I managed two laps with McCallen fastest as expected but I was second quickest so I felt good about that. That's because I knew where I was going. I dropped down the practice leaderboard over the next few days as the non-locals learned the course.

There were five locals making our debuts and we all had the same goal; reach the finish line, without making a fool of ourselves. By that I mean you may think you have a chance to get in the top six but end up something like 36th. As it turned out we all did quite well. Gilmour finished third in his race ahead of Simon Beck while David Black was just inside the top 10. I ended up seventh in mine having been fifth on the first lap. Brian fell at the Waterworks having looked strong up until that point while Trevor Burden was in fifth place at the end of the first lap but then his chain broke going over the top of Crosby Hill. We all achieved so much that year as it was about learning and taking that experience into the next.

I kept the same bike for the next year in which I managed to win my first replica. I pulled off a great deal when I bought a big tank from Andy

Bassett. He'd used it to finish 9th in the previous year's Lightweight race and offered to sell it to me for £100. I took his hand off and he took my money. So the following year I kept it hidden, I didn't tell anybody about it until Friday night practice because by then it would be too late for anybody else to get one made. I also wanted to try it to make sure it worked with breathers and what have you. It was that big it meant I didn't have to stop for fuel and over the four laps I didn't. So I finished 15th in the Lightweight, an improvement of ten places on the year before and then I sold the tank to a guy called Bernie Webster at the end of the race for £95. Therefore, it only cost me a fiver to use.

I didn't want to do the TT until I'd won a Manx Grand Prix race. However, things didn't work out like that. In 1996 I rented a 250 Yamaha from Padgett's for one race only, the Lightweight. I took out a three-year bank loan to pay for it and finished second, less than five seconds down on the winner. By 1997 I had some backing from the Manton Group and was going well in the MGP Lightweight race. I was in second place around twenty seconds down on the leader Garry Linham. My visor had been misting up but by lap three it had cleared so I'd reduced the gap to thirteen seconds at Glen Helen. I was riding at number one on the road. There wasn't another bike anywhere near me, I was out on my own. As I blasted along the Cronk y Voddy straight everything looked good until all of a sudden the engine cut out. I pulled over onto the roadside thinking maybe the chain had come off when I noticed the kill switch was turned off. One of those things that can happen when you're riding hard. It's also happened to Robert Dunlop and Ian Lougher, plus always seemed to happen on the Hondas more than the TZs.

During those few agonising seconds on the side of the road, four bikes flew past. This compounded my situation further. I got going again but my head was done in. I ran wide at a few places so I had a quiet word with myself.

"Pull yourself together. This isn't going to happen today,"

I got back up to fifth and shared the fastest lap time with Norman Gordon from Northern Ireland.

A few weeks later I was in the Scarborough paddock with Steve Brown, who was my sponsor with the Manton Group. He asked what I had planned for the following year.

"Well, after this year's disappointment, I would like to do one more year at the Manx and then maybe the TT"

"Well, if that's what you want to do, that's absolutely great. I wish you all the best," said Steve. *"However, I can't get time off for the Manx next year. I know that in advance but if you were prepared to do TT, I could be there. Plus, I know Steve Manton's buying a brand new 250 and you could be on it."*

I said I'd have a little think about it but even after two or three minutes, I realised I had to go with him because I didn't have another bike for the Manx. As it worked out the MGP was a wet one, the Lightweight race was a two lap dash on very damp roads. Tommy Diver won it with Richard 'Milky' Quayle second and I remember standing on the grid thinking to myself, '*I'm quite glad I'm not here racing today!*'

It had also been rather damp for my first TT race, the Lightweight, a few weeks earlier which Joey Dunlop famously won. It was my first ride on a brand new 250cc bike and at a cost of 18 and a half grand there was no way I wanted to take any risks on it. I just had to get it home in one piece. I finished 17th so won a bronze replica but I didn't get the opportunity to get my teeth into the race, not many of us did really. Luckily I had another run on it in the Senior on the Friday, which was in great conditions and was most enjoyable.

You may get two or three big chances in the Manx and if it doesn't happen, it might never happen. The likes of Bob Jackson, Gordon Pantall, Derek Young, Mick Robinson, fine Manx Grand Prix riders amongst many others who should have won it, not once but several times, except that luck wasn't there on the day for them.

I was back again in '99 for the TT but crashed at Union Mills on Thursday afternoon practice. I'd been out on the 125 for a couple of laps and then I had to do a plug chop so if you're doing that you have to push the bike back up that big long return road. As I was doing this Steve came

"Racing was a very expensive pastime. Up until this point I had been working for the past 15 years as a labourer for the Isle of Man Highway Board. The wages were poor but somehow I found the money. I don't know how but I did."

BARRY WOOD

running into vision urging me to hurry as there was only four minutes until the flag went out to finish the session. I was fairly knackered having had to push the bike back plus it was a hot day as well. As I was about to get on the machine I was told they'd not had the tyre warmers on. We were running slicks. Therefore I took it easy down to Quarterbridge and the run through Braddan Bridge. Going up the straight I simulated a couple of little high speed weaves and it felt okay so I thought I should be alright. However, as I negotiated Union Mills, the whole lot just folded beneath me which meant I had a first ever ride in the helicopter.

Racing was a very expensive pastime. Up until this point I had been working for the past 15 years as a labourer for the Isle of Man Highway Board. The wages were poor but somehow I found the money. I don't know how but I did. At the end of the '90s I became a full-time taxi driver, thankfully just at the right time as there was something of an economic and building boom on the Island. All of a sudden, I was working twice the hours I had been used to but earning a lot more money as I was making the most of things by putting in fourteen hours a day and having just one day off every fortnight. The incentive was there as all I wanted to do was go racing.

I had some help from the Manton Group, Steve Brown, people like that. He was a great help sorting the ride on his bike. From the outside it looked like I was doing well getting these seats but most people didn't know I still needed to find big money to pay the running costs for the bikes. When I crashed them, I got massive bills. It wasn't the case where the sponsor was picking up the tab. Folk are often unaware of the real situation. Eventually I decided I was happier funding on my own although it probably held me back.

The Foot and Mouth crisis which cancelled the TT in 2001 was something of a blessing in disguise for me. Of course I'd have preferred to have raced but as it was, the money I'd saved up for that year meant I had more to spend in 2002. I managed to get out twice in Ireland at the Cookstown 100 and Skerries 100. So I had all this money and wondered what the hell I was going to do. I saw a Yamaha R1 for sale at a local dealer so I bought it. It was in immaculate condition, very reasonably priced, so the plan was to use it as a road bike to ride out on and next year, use it in the Production TT. So that's what I did. The truth is I struggled to get to grips with it. I also picked up a Honda CBR 400 which I was told had been a previous race winner but by the time I bought it all the best parts had been taken out. I was about ninth overall in practice and unfortunately, in the last session, it blew itself to bits on the Mountain. I managed to borrow an engine but there was no time to test it. As I left the line the bike just wouldn't rev properly and I was the first retirement on Bray Hill. So 2002 wasn't a great year for me, it was only after that things started to improve.

People may wonder why I kept going back, kept ploughing money in, kept spending every spare moment I had on my bikes and the simple answer is the Mountain circuit. Once you've raced it at speed it has you hooked which was certainly true in my case. Even though sometimes you know you haven't a cat in hell's chance of winning against the big boys and all the backing they have, you are still drawn to it. It's an incredible feeling.

By 2003 it was all over for the 250 class with Bruce Anstey winning the last one the year before so I knew I had to change. The 400 had been a disaster for me so personally I knew things would have to be different from now on. I bought a brand new Yamaha R6 which meant I could do the Junior TT and also race in the Production 600. They were still allowing 250s to race but in mixed class with no separate prize. Paul Owen was starting near me, so we chatted on the grid, with him saying he would continue to ride the 250 as long as he could whereas because I was paying for this myself, I really had no choice, I was going to have to ride 600s for the next three years. I just wanted to race on the TT course. That was my sole purpose in life even though I was a regular Top 30 finisher including a couple of Top 20 positions with no hope of standing on the rostrum.

I had a few bronze replicas, always wanted a silver one but missed out by about 12 seconds, something like that. That was the closest I came. My fastest lap had been over 116 mph on a standard 105 horsepower bike. Another ambition was to do a 120 mph lap and I thought if I had a bigger bike then I should be able to do it. So I bought a new model Yamaha R1, the type with the exhaust under the seat and entered the Superbike race for 2006. Unfortunately, a poor decision on my behalf because even though it would be a six lap race, I never even gave a thought to wheel changes. You had to have quick release swing arms but this had never crossed my mind. When I competed in the Senior on the 250 I never needed to. Buying one was going to cost well over a thousand pounds and even that was a used second hand one which I just couldn't afford. I was advised to use a hard compound back tyre to have any chance of completing six laps which it may have done but not at the pace we were on. I did just under 118mph from a standing start on the first lap but on the third the back end of the bike suddenly stepped out with no warning at the 11th Milestone, sending me off. I was very lucky to get away with that. I can just remember sliding along the road. It happened so quickly and it's funny what goes through your mind, mainly *'I hope I don't hit anything hard.'* I slid along the bales against the wall and was then bounced into the road while the bike carried on ahead of me. I managed to get to my knees and crawl off the track. So I'm lying there and with the pitter patter of marshalls feet getting louder. I was soon standing and helped into the field to take the helicopter to hospital but I was under a lot of surveillance all of the time. The medics saw I'd broken my collarbone but weren't sure if there may be some more injuries they couldn't see so I was sent to hospital for an X-ray. They were worried I may have broken my neck but the collarbone was hampering their view so I was told

'this is going to hurt so scream as much as you want'

but as they pulled it down it wasn't that bad. The good news was my neck wasn't broken. I wasn't in hospital for long however it meant I couldn't ride my 600 which was a real blow as I'd gone well on that in practice. However, it was a lucky escape considering the damage to the bike.

The Centenary TT of 2007 was something I was never going to miss. I had the same bike but completely rebuilt plus I needed new leathers, boots, gloves, helmet, after everything had been destroyed in the 11th Milestone accident. I had an orange and white colour scheme. I raced at a few other events as you needed the Mountain course licence which had just been introduced. I'd competed at the Jurby Road course the week before TT practice began and had just missed out on the podium in the big bike races against good opposition in Paul Hunt and Nigel Beattie so I was happy with things. Then it all went to hell in the first practice. I had a major accident, life threatening, which meant I never raced again. I thought about carrying on but when I added up all it had cost me financially over the years, plus it was the third time I had broken my back, so I knew the odds were stacked against me. It was all over.

It was an untimed session so there was no need for speed. The first lap I'd been a little bit rusty which was to be expected but everything started to click on the second. I was on slick tyres, feeling good and managed to pass a few I didn't expect to. We'd been warned it could be wet possibly around half an hour or so after the session was underway. As we came into Ramsey there were a few drops of rain on my screen and visor. So I slowed down, went into the hairpin and just ahead was newcomer Antonio Maeso from Spain. I slowly crept past him thinking *'let's just get home, it's been a decent first night'*. I then had a slide coming into the Waterworks and the back end stepped out. As that happened I involuntarily wound the throttle on, it was just a reflex reaction but the back found some grip and that sent me plus the bike barrelling into the corner flat in first gear, which is probably about 90 miles an hour, on a wet road, on slick tyres. If I had braked heavily then I would have gone down big time. It's funny what goes through your mind in those moments. I just tried to ride it out. However both myself and the bike were flung into space. There's no other way to describe it.

It was the shock loading when hitting the bales and wall that caused most of my injuries. I was flung one way, the bike went in the other direction and came to rest about 30 yards away. They found that but they couldn't find me. I could hear them shouting but they seemed a long way away. I was in a lot of bracken and gorse. There was a cold feeling in my back and my left leg was bent around behind me. I could taste blood in my mouth which was worrying plus I knew you're not meant to but in a panic, I managed to take my helmet off. As it turned out I had shattered my dentures, cutting my tongue and lips so that's what caused the bleeding. I was just very relieved the R1 hadn't landed on top of me.

Eventually I was found and it was two good friends of mine, Allan Brew and Jim Weeks, which was comforting. They called my Mum, she was at the paddock and already knew there'd been a bad accident having watched the helicopter go out. These were the early days of instant communication where people texted their friends if something had happened and the word was back in the Grandstand within minutes. Before the authorities could find her to let her know what had happened she'd heard somebody mentioning my name and how it had been a bad one in relation to the crash. I was later told poor Maseo was very distraught when he got back to the paddock, he thought he'd witnessed a fatality.

Financially things could have been a lot worse but, from when I became a taxi driver, I've always had my own personal insurance. I was only in hospital for just over a week but when I went home I couldn't work for four months. I had a full body cast and because I'd also broken my arm I couldn't use crutches or other aids. It was a dark time for me. I was housebound for several weeks. Eventually, I just tried to walk around the block with the dog. It was that and getting to the pub that kept me going.

The accident was life changing. I lost two inches in height as a result. I'm five foot eight now whereas I used to be five foot 10. I still have aches and pains but absolutely no regrets. I was 43 years old at that time and although I was getting quicker every year, my best days had gone in some ways but at the same time I had still been committed to the Classic races. I had actually said ahead of 2006 if I had a good run on the R1 and achieved my ambitions I would probably quit the TT but then after the accident I didn't want things to finish like that. So I came back in 2007, exactly the same thing happened, but I couldn't afford to race again in 2008. So my decision to retire was partly mental, partly physical and a lot financial.

Whereas the TT hadn't gone that well for me at times, the Manx Grand Prix did. To win a MGP race would be a dream come true. I'd come close, had a few thirds and a few seconds over the years, so there was always a chance but it was tough with plenty of fast guys around the likes of Bob and 'Bud' Jackson, Bill Swallow or Roy Richardson and you have to match these people on the day if you're to succeed.

In the Classic Lightweight Manx Grand Prix race in 1999 I was on the 250cc Suzuki and seemed to have a safe second place. I had a board at the end of the third lap that said *'P2 minus 25'* and I knew it would be Roy. When I arrived at Glen Helen I was still second but the gap was now just one second. Richardson was having problems. My next signal was at Rhen Cullen and there it was, a single finger held up by a pal of mine, Steve Parkinson.

I felt good for a brief moment but then you're always thinking something's going to go wrong, especially on a temperamental Classic bike. I just thought about getting it home which I did. It all came together. To this day I know that my good fortune was Roy's misfortune.

I went back the following year with a different mindset. It's like anything; once you've done it you know you can do it again. That's what I did in 2000 as I won the race once more but this time I didn't need others misfortune to do so. Alan 'Bud' Jackson was second with Roy third and my fastest lap this time was the same as Roy's had been the year before while he was leading.

It was the best time of my life. An ambition realised not just for me but my Mum also. I can't sum up how emotional I feel when I think back to those times. Maybe lots of local people

don't have quite as much passion for the Isle of Man and what it means to be Manx as I do. I've always felt that way. I've been brought up by my Mum to be proud to be Manx. There was no prouder Manxman when I stood on top of the podium at the TT Grandstand as the Manx national anthem, *'O Land of our Birth'*, was blasted out over the speakers.

After winning that race people were expecting to see me celebrating in the beer tent but I'd promised to do the pits for Brian Mateer in that afternoon's Junior race so I had to be sober to do that! I wouldn't have swapped that situation either. It was good to help others as they had helped me. Also, I had a transit van with Barry Wood Racing on it. The last thing I wanted to do was drive over the limit past the police station which was fifty yards away. Later when I drove up our road back to the house the neighbours were out clapping and cheering; what a feeling that was. Totally unforgettable.

The phone at home didn't stop ringing either with congratulatory calls as there weren't so many mobiles back then. We went to a nearby pub, the Cat with No Tail, and we were treated to a three course meal by the manager Anthony Atkinson who had also helped out with sponsorship. It's those little things you never forget and make it all worthwhile.

Barry still lives in the Isle of Man where he continues to drive a taxi. Unofficially he helps newcomers to the Manx Grand Prix by taking them on laps of the TT circuit in his car and runs the Mountain Memories Facebook group. His mother Babara passed away in 2018.

ACKNOWLEDGEMENTS

There are a few people I need to thank in helping this project see the light of day. Heather Bowen, Chris Boyde, Chris and Tony Briggs, Simon Crellin, Jules Gammond, Shaun Hogg, John McAvoy, Peter and Emily Moore, Don Morley, Amy Mulhern, Kit Nelson, James Proudfoot and Michael Rutter all of whom have played varying parts in supporting me along the way plus of course the riders themselves for giving up their time to tell their tales. I think they all deserve a dedicated book about themselves and maybe this will help lead to that happening. The majority of the interviews took place during the recent Covid pandemic the exceptions being Giacomo Agostini when I spoke to him 20 years ago while Murray Walker was a special guest for the Manx Grand Prix in 2002 and I had the great privilege of spending time and working with him during the event. Every rider featured in this book has either won a TT or a Manx Grand Prix with the exception of Murray Walker, who is the son of a TT winner. Work's already begun on Isle of Man TT Greats Volume 2, which will be more solo riders but the plan is to have future volumes dedicated to sidecars and non-racers like team bosses etc as there are stories aplenty about the Isle of Man TT, the greatest race meeting in the world.

ABOUT THE AUTHOR

Dave Moore is a journalist and motorsport commentator who specialises in motorcycle racing. His broadcasting career began 30 years ago and his first race behind the microphone was in 1999. Born and bred in the Isle of Man he has been the main TV commentator on the TT since 2018 and was behind the mic when the event created history in 2022 when it was broadcast live around the world for the very first time. His commentary portfolio also includes the North West 200, Ulster Grand Prix, British Rally championship, British Motocross championship, Super Enduro World Championship, British Rallycross championship, Porsche Carrera Cup to name but a few.